the HYBRID ELECTRIC HOME

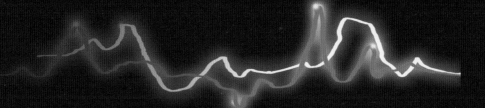

CLEAN • EFFICIENT • PROFITABLE

CRAIG TOEPFER

4880 Lower Valley Road • Atglen, Pennsylvania 19310

Schiffer Books are available at special discounts for bulk purchases for sales promotions or premiums. Special editions, including personalized covers, corporate imprints, and excerpts can be created in large quantities for special needs. For more information contact the publisher:

Published by Schiffer Publishing Ltd.
4880 Lower Valley Road
Atglen, PA 19310
Phone: (610) 593-1777; Fax: (610) 593-2002
E-mail: Info@schifferbooks.com

For the largest selection of fine reference books on this and related subjects, please visit our web site at
www.schifferbooks.com
We are always looking for people to write books on new and related subjects. If you have an idea for a book please contact us at the above address.

This book may be purchased from the publisher.
Include $5.00 for shipping.
Please try your bookstore first.
You may write for a free catalog.

In Europe, Schiffer books are distributed by
Bushwood Books
6 Marksbury Ave.
Kew Gardens
Surrey TW9 4JF England
Phone: 44 (0) 20 8392 8585; Fax: 44 (0) 20 8392 9876
E-mail: info@bushwoodbooks.co.uk
Website: www.bushwoodbooks.co.uk

Copyright © 2010 by Craig Toepfer
Library of Congress Control Number: 2009935103

Designed by RoS
Type set in BellCent SubCap BTt/Arial

ISBN: 978-0-7643-3403-0
Printed in China

DEDICATION

To Hailee Victoria and Jakob Richard, their parents, and people of good will everywhere.

PREFACE

This book was written to share a lifetime of experience restoring, installing, maintaining, designing, engineering, promoting, and living with equipment for producing electricity from wind and solar energy for private use. A walk through history from early beginnings, including a significant segment that has been lost to time, will hopefully make electricity a little friendlier and more understandable for everyone. The success of this book will be measured by how many readers come to the conclusion that it is not only possible, but easy, to produce electricity for modern needs and conveniences, using a small amount of the solar and wind energy available to each of us continuously and predictably.

ACKNOWLEDGMENTS

Along the path to getting this material into book form, many people have directly and indirectly contributed through their friendship, support, and shared experiences. None was more helpful than Chris Gillis, who called me out of the blue one day and introduced himself. He was writing a book on wind energy and found my name associated with wind energy somewhere in the past. He had heard about the wind electric industry in the 1930s and 1940s and wanted to know more. Since wind energy people are always happy to share, I helped him out as best I could. Well, the help must have worked, because he now has the wind bug. On the way, he stopped by to look at my wind memorabilia that had been collecting dust for a while. He was so excited and enthusiastic about co-authoring a book just on this subject, he got me thinking about it. A few months and conversations later, I agreed to take on the extra time and effort to co-author a book—it was meant to happen. Gradually, Chris convinced me to be the sole author, and he would help me as much as he could. He is the editor of an important trade journal and has skills that can be a big help to a freshman author. Chris and his wife, Theresa, are every bit as responsible for this book through their efforts and encouragement as I am. I can't thank them enough.

I first got to know Marcellus L. Jacobs in 1975, when I bought from him one of his famous original Jacobs Wind Electric Plants. In the ensuing years, M. L., as everyone knew him, provided typewritten technical support letters, and we occasionally visited each other. He was in Fort Myers, Florida, planning his comeback with a new larger wind generator for modern times and needs. I was in Michigan buying, selling, collecting, restoring, and installing every antique Jacobs Wind Electric Plant that I could get my hands on. In 1980, M. L. moved to Minneapolis to set up production on his new 10 kilowatt wind machine with financial support from Control Data. When the first units were nearing completion, he asked me to help him put together the installation manual, and I went to work at his shop for several weeks. We had lunch and dinner together most days and the experiences and stories all came out. I returned to work for him a few years later when he wanted to develop a standalone battery hybrid wind and solar electric plant. One of the things so inspiring about M. L. was the original Jacobs Wind Electric Plant itself. To watch one of his wind machines operate in a strong breeze from the base of the tower, or even from afar, is a marvel. But more importantly, when it is yours and it operates reliably, silently and efficiently, day after day, you truly begin to understand how challenging harnessing the energy in the wind can be and how perfectly Jacobs met this challenge. The same was true for his new machine. While listening to him describe how to do something to one of his talented engineers, you understood that he knew exactly what he was talking about. You also knew that reliable performance drove all his technical decisions. In the final analysis, he taught me the value of value, inspired me in many ways to do the best and right thing, and gave me the foundation to be able to tell this story.

Before joining Jacobs in Minneapolis, I had the pleasure of working with a fun and talented group of engineers at Windworks in Wisconsin. Founded by Hans Meyer, with encouragement and support from Buckminster Fuller, Windworks accomplished more with less than any corporation could be expected to do. After successfully stimulating interest in sustainable energy, Windworks was the first to develop the concept and equipment to electronically connect wind generators and solar panels to the electric grid. As a result, they expanded the opportunities for wind and solar energy significantly. Under contract to the Department of Energy, Windworks would design and build 30 innovative 10-kilowatt wind generators and put them in service throughout Wisconsin and around the country at government test facilities and electric utilities. Thanks to Hans and the Windworks staff for the great experiences and keeping me involved in the wind business at an important time.

Although I started with a good understanding of electricity in general and wind energy in particular, I was interested in gaining a deeper insight into the Delco-Light and other farm electric plants. My first stop was to visit Curt Dalton, the archivist at Dayton History in Dayton, Ohio. Curt was kind enough to open parts of the archive related to Charles Kettering and Delco, copy and photograph information, and guide me in my quest for information. I soon visited the Scharchburg Archives at Kettering University in Flint, Michigan. Archivists David White and Jane Gunderson were equally helpful in sharing documents, copying and photographing key documents, and encouraging me in my quest. I also gained an appreciation for organizations, like Dayton History and the Scharchburg Archives, involved in the active preservation of our common history and significant achievements.

The best was yet to come. In my quest for information, I became aware of a man called Dr. Delco, who everyone said was a great source of information. With a little digging, I found Dr. Delco, whose real name is Wayne Sphar, in Avella, Pennsylvania, and gave him a call. Wayne collected Delco-Light plants for over 40 years with a vigor that was greater than that with which I collected wind generators, so we hit it off. Not only that, he operated a private Delco-Light museum that was filled with Delco farm electric equipment with everything in operating order. He sold the equipment a few years back and it is currently in storage. At any rate, I drove to Avella and spent a day with Wayne and his wife, Nancy, to share stories about hunting for farm electric equipment. Wayne also showed me his vast collection of literature, manuals, newsletters, and memorabilia about Delco-Light and the entire range of related products. I was astounded at what I saw and amazed that knowledge of the once-large farm electric plant business has been lost in time. Subsequently, Wayne sent me his entire collection and asked me to help him make this information available to as many people as possible and to find a permanent home for it. It is really a remarkable collection and I have had many of the documents photographed, some of which can be enjoyed in this book. I will be developing a website, www.doctordelco.com, to make this information available to others. Thanks, Wayne, for sharing your knowledge.

A special thanks for professional assistance goes to these friends and neighbors: Dave Devore of Keepsake Video (www.dcdstudios.com), Michael Hough of Ivory Photo (www.ivoryphoto.com), Alicia Ryan-Loos of Purple Frog Photography (www.purplefrogphotography.com), and Bruce and Jim at Rubin-Cordaro Design (www.rubincordaro.com) who have been helping me put my best foot forward for twenty years.

Finally, many thanks go to my family and friends for their support, encouragement, and motivation to tell a story that needs to be told.

Contents

INTRODUCTION

Electricity is a natural force that has become an important presence in human life wherever we are and at virtually every moment in time. It serves people, communities, municipalities, commerce, industry, government, and nations. It surrounds us no matter where we are—at home, work, play, in public, and in our travels. Despite this, electricity is still a mysterious force and most attempts to describe it factually in an understandable manner become complicated and leave unanswered questions in our minds. Perhaps it is because the beginning of human understanding of electricity is fairly recent, and its migration into all aspects of our lives has been growing over an even shorter period of time. Or maybe it is because we have not been able to fully understand the complexity of how it functions. Whatever the reason, the truly important thing to consider is what we have learned from our experiences and how we are going to apply it towards a better and more efficient force for improving our lives.

The purpose of this book is to make electricity a little more friendly and understandable, to learn about the important devices that make electricity possible, to examine how our electric supply system came to be what it is today, and to apply this understanding to shape the future electric system to better serve our needs.

Today, life without electricity is a nearly unimaginable concept for most people. Throughout most of human history, our experience with electricity was limited to the awesome majesty of lightning and the simple curiosity of static effects. The beginning of our formal understanding of electricity began quite by accident by a professor of anatomy in 1791. For the next 70 years, electricity was confined to the laboratories in colleges and universities around the world as we struggled to gain a better understanding of this amazing force. The later half of the 19th century witnessed practical applications and demonstrations and the development of equipment to produce and use electricity. From meager beginnings at the turn of the 20th century, electricity has extended its reach into every segment of our society and into our lives in unforeseen ways and in seemingly inexhaustible amounts.

The story of the transformation from simple beginnings of intellectual curiosity to a powerful force in the daily lives of everyone is a fascinating journey and can provide insights for the future. Given the state of the planet at the dawn of the new millennium, a review of where we are, how we got here, and the lessons along the pathway can help guide us in choosing and developing an electric system in the future that is dramatically better in responsibly serving us.

My definition of electricity is quite simple and needs no formulas. "Electricity is a medium for connecting energy sources with our wishes - to perform work, fulfill a need, or satisfy a want," or in simple notation: energy sources > electricity > work/needs/wants.

A medium is a "middle state or condition," and in the case of electricity, the connection between an energy source and our wishes travels at the speed of light. Understanding the energy sources and how we use them is important in understanding electricity. When we wish to see in the dark, a flip of the light switch causes a piece of coal to be burned somewhere to fill the room with light. Electricity is the middle state, the intermediate condition that served as the means to make that happen. Today we see the familiar pieces of the electric supply network all around us, from the meter on our homes to the power distribution lines, substations, transmission lines, and occasional power plant. In our homes and businesses, we are surrounded by electrical switches, outlets, and devices within reach wherever we are.

Understanding electricity, as I have defined it, involves a journey. The first step is to understand the sources and various forms of energy available to us. We will proceed to a historical study of the development of the essential components of electric technology and set the stage for using it. All of this brings us to an analysis of how these events came to impact our lives, and leaves us with the question: How do we get "it" and how do we use "it"? Knowing how we got to this point, though, is not enough. Using what we have learned and applying it to strengthen and improve the electric supply network in the future is an obvious obligation for all and should be a national priority.

As you will see, our journey leads us to the re-development of private power plants for homes and businesses in farm and rural settings, community and municipal systems using local or regional resources, and strengthening the urban central station system through logical choices, promoting efficiency, and solar air conditioning.

For several reasons, the starting point for me in this journey is the year 1776. First of all, this is the beginning of our national journey of common purpose, and energy and electricity will become inextricably intertwined with the American experience. Second, at this point in history our energy use was a very small fraction of what we use today - individually and collectively. Additionally, no one could have possibly imagined at that point, despite Benjamin Franklin's experiments with lightening 24 years earlier, what profound impacts energy and electricity would have in the development of our nation. And finally, the American experience was paralleled in other developed nations and served as a model to lead similar development in emerging economies.

From this starting point, we will examine our energy sources and forms of energy which lead us backwards in time briefly—-540 million years—before we proceed to the development of electric technology, the path into our lives, and a discussion of what we learned and what is the most rational way to proceed. The understanding of electricity grew from simple beginnings into a very few technological devices that would change society profoundly. I am of the opinion that there are only five basic pieces of electrical equipment that are necessary to be able to bring energy sources to you in the useable form of electricity, and of course a lot of wires. They are:

• Primary electrochemical cell or battery

• Electromagnetic dynamo or generator and motor

• Secondary electrochemical cell or rechargeable battery

• Alternating current transformer

• Photovoltaic cell or solar panel

These are all reasonably simple devices that are easy to understand and familiar to us. It is a worthwhile effort to understand how these pieces evolved into our electric supply network or hold promise for the future.

As electric technology evolved, the first applications were privately or municipally owned power systems, such as street lights, trolleys, mines, ships, farms, businesses, and industries. The electric industry business model was making and selling equipment to satisfy a growing market demand. This would not always be the case.

The concept of making and selling electrical equipment received competition from a new idea: the selling of electricity which would ultimately dominate and take over. Thomas Edison's first direct current power stations lost a technology battle with the "new" Westinghouse/Tesla alternating current system and the future was set. The "natural monopoly" for electricity with regulation to "prevent excesses" was established. In modern times, a significant majority, more than 75 percent, of residential, commercial, and industrial customers are supplied by a regional investor-owned electric utility operating in an "assigned" service territory. Subjected to federal and state regulation throughout history, the investor-owned utilities have been struggling with de-regulation and privatization in recent years. Municipal systems and rural electric cooperatives provide electric service to the balance of electric customers in the United States. Regardless of where you live though, if you want electricity there is only one choice.

For many years, electricity was only available to city dwellers as envious farm families longed to have electricity, too. This demand for electricity in rural and remote areas inspired Charles Kettering to develop the Delco-Light farm electric plant. This hybrid power system composed of an engine generator set and a battery included electric lights, water pumps for running water, appliances for convenience, and motors to power the farm. The genset was used to recharge a large battery and would start and stop automatically when the battery was discharged and charged respectively. A large number of farms produced their own power, initially with fuels and later with wind generators. Several entrepreneurs manufactured, sold, installed, and serviced wind electric generators in the windy Great Plains to reduce or eliminate the use of fuel. The farm electric plant business grew dramatically, even during the earliest years of the Great Depression. But things were about to change.

Prior to the depression, electric companies were "consolidating" and growing fewer in number. During this time, the federal government began its involvement with electricity by controlling the nation's waterways and building large dams and moving onto the regulation of the electric "monopolies." This involvement expanded with the Tennessee Valley Authority in Appalachia, the Bureau of Reclamation west of the Mississippi, and the misguided Rural Electrification Act, which destroyed the thriving farm power plant industry. In the post-World War II years, the government's involvement increased dramatically with the Atomic Energy Agency and the "Peaceful Atom Program." The environmental movement and the oil crisis of the mid-1970s changed the discussion and broadened the horizon for energy policy. During this same period, mission conflict led to the Atomic Energy Commission's demise and re-emergence a decade later as the Department of Energy. Today, a shrinking number of interconnected, centralized, quasi-regulated investor-owned electric utilities, some divided into related services, provide a complex solution to a simple question for most users — Which one provides my electricity?

What we do with the electricity once we have it is another story. From the incandescent light bulb to a myriad of devices to perform an amazing array of tasks, the types of equipment that deliver our wishes are almost limitless, including heating water, keeping food fresh and cooking it, washing clothes, entertaining, keeping cool on hot days, brushing teeth, and drying hair. Each need or task has electrical equipment associated with it, and these devices are called "utilization equipment," but are more commonly referred to as electrical appliances or devices. As I write, I am certain that someone somewhere is developing a new device that uses electricity to make life better. I am just as certain that 10 years from now, and 50 years further, someone will find a new way to have electricity perform some useful task or fulfill some unimagined need.

1. *What we have learned from our experiences and how we proceed can be profoundly influenced by the decisions we make today and in the coming few decades.*

An obvious lesson is that one size does not fit all. Our national electric supply network took a major wrong turn when the Rural Electrification Act extended the city electric system to the remotest parts of our country. Even the electric companies thought this was ridiculous at the time, but they did eventually accept the increased demand. The nature of science, societal influences, and human behavior drive us towards a single "best" solution - the lightest, fastest, most efficient, and cost-effective. It should be clear that the best solution is determined by the circumstances. It should be equally clear that there are a broad range of circumstances and thus a variety of best solutions for each. For instance, the best solution for personal mobility in the major urban centers — the subways of New York, London, Paris, Moscow, and others — does not work so well for our fellow citizens in rural environments, such as Iowa or Montana. The same is true for electricity.

2. The second major lesson to be learned is that the dominant portion of our electric supply network is based on principles antithetical to our economic system using assumptions that have been proven wrong.

Giving "natural monopoly" status to privately-owned electric utilities, with the added benefit of "regulation" effectively eliminating both "competition" and "risk," was a significant mistake. The result has been imprudent investment in generating capacity, encouragement of inefficiency and waste, and the disregard or subjugation of "meeting market demands and improving the lives of consumers." The government role in the electric supply network made this complex situation more complicated and makes a compelling argument for an honest review and intelligent restructuring. There are several models on how this matter has been addressed in similar circumstances - rail, water, phone, highways, police, fire - at different times and in different countries. The path forward must inevitably revisit the private and public relationship and how each can best serve our needs in a manner consistent with our beliefs, principles, and shared goals in the future.

3. Another lesson is that sometimes events with enduring effects can be determined by limited knowledge or matters of lesser status.

The debate between Edison and Westinghouse/ Tesla over direct current versus alternating current had unintended consequences for a person using electricity. What was good for generating, transmitting, and distributing electricity led to alternating current totally dominating the entire electric network, including being brought into our homes for all of our electrical devices to use. Ironically, Edison was right on the safety issue. In its most common form, 120 volts, alternating current is less safe and is potentially lethal. Given a fresh start, a powerful argument could be made that direct current at a safe voltage would be superior for use in our homes and businesses. To make matters worse, alternating current is the most significant impediment to the broad scale use of solar, wind, and other variable energy sources today.

The path to developing a more thoughtful electric supply system can be both exciting and rewarding, while providing immense benefits for everyone. It begins with the simple idea that energy is all around us and the medium of electricity can allow each of us to meet our energy needs harmoniously with our environment. Resisting change is not an option, and delaying the transition to clean efficient energy technologies is not a good alternative. It is time to begin to enjoy the transition to truly give electric power to the people.

In a final note, the most difficult task for a technical writer is to make science understandable for all. I promise to use words to the maximum and limit formulas and data to a minimum in frequency and scope and to use small numbers. Please bear with me through those moments when this is not possible. In conjunction, I have chosen to use average or median values and general principles to guide the technical content wherever possible and leave the extremes and discontinuities open for discussion at a different time.

Chapter 1

ENERGY SOURCES, FORMS, and MEDIUMS

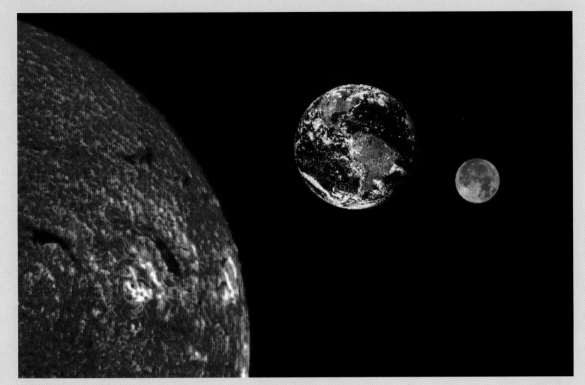

The sources of all our energy

In the winter months of 1776, the founding fathers, like most everyone else in the colonies, used wood, plant oils, and animal oils as their primary sources of energy. Wood was used for heat on cold nights, cooking year round, and an occasional warm bath. Plant and animal oils were used to light the dark with open flame candles and oil lamps - the glass lamp chimney to control combustion and increase light would be invented seven years later. In both cases, it was important to be near the heat and light source. In the case of candles and oil lamps, they had to be carried from room to room.

Winter would give way to longer days and warmer temperatures. March would come in like a lion and go out a lamb, yielding to April showers and, of course, May flowers, and finally hot summer days. In June, waking to the light of an "early" sunrise, walking about on the earth, and returning home with the moon above combine with the experiences of the past months to confront them with and confirm what we all have come to know and understand today: There are only three sources of energy available to us – the sun, earth, and moon.

Between them, they offer 11 forms of energy from which to choose. We convert these energy sources into five intermediate states, or energy mediums, using a few simple devices. In the electrical medium, energy is converted to electricity and transmitted though wires for use. We convert it again using utilization equipment or electrical appliances or devices to perform work, fulfill a need, or satisfy a want. And thus, my definition of electricity is fulfilled and the sun, earth, and moon can be connected with useful work, essential needs, and important wants as shown.

Before we try to understand the essential electrical devices and how they evolved to fit together and into our lives, it is important to begin with a basic understanding of our sources and forms of energy. Of our three sole sources of energy — the sun, the earth, and the moon — the sun is by far the greatest source. It is 5,000 times greater than the earth and moon combined. The obvious starting point to learn about energy is the sun. I have divided the sun's energy into two separate categories — permanent and temporary — and will deal with them independently.

I classify the radiant light energy from the sun as permanent because it is a steady and constant flow that has been coming to earth since its birth a little over 4.5 billion years ago and is expected to continue

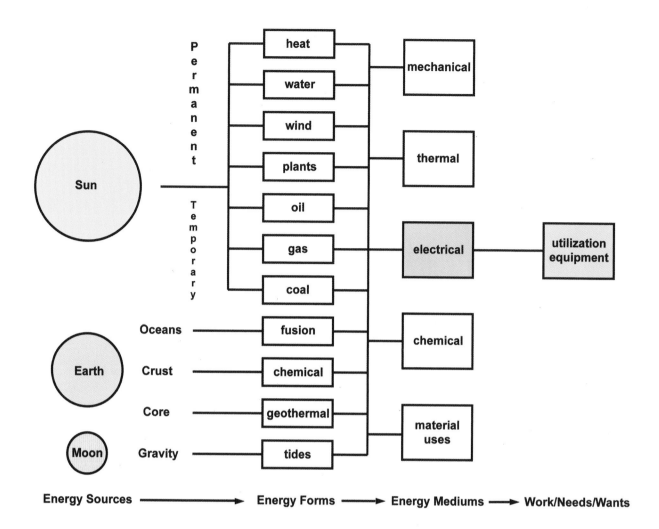

to do so for another 5 billion years or so before it runs out of fuel. I think it would be fair to call that permanent for all practical purposes. The amount of radiant energy arriving at the earth, given our relative distance and size, is a miniscule amount of the energy produced continuously by the sun.

A few small facts to consider are:

• The earth is between 7,900 and 7,926 miles in diameter. The diameter at the equator is a little larger than the polar diameter, more like a pumpkin than a ball.

• The earth orbits the sun at a distance that varies slightly, between 91 and 94.5 million miles depending on the time of year.

• The sun is 864,938 miles in diameter, which is 109 times the diameter of the earth.

• About 1.3 million earths could fit within the sun.

• The sun has 99.8 percent of the mass in our entire solar system.

• The sun weighs 333,000 times as much as the earth.

• The energy arriving on the earth's projected area of 49,178,150 square miles represents only a miniscule amount of the sun's total energy, but is 15,000 times our global energy needs.

It's so familiar in our lives that it's easy to overlook the incredible immensity of the sun's energy. Based on the facts above, it's clear that "immense" is not an overstatement, but an ineffective term for the actual magnitude of it. The sun radiates light energy in all directions, a tiny fraction of which is directed at earth 93 million miles away. It arrives continuously on the half of our planet that is facing the sun at any given moment. Nearly 30 percent of the light energy is reflected back into space by our protective atmosphere and never arrives at the earth's surface. As we will come to understand, this is a very good bit of fortune. The balance of the solar energy reaching the planet takes on four forms, which I will call heat, water, wind, and plants.

Nearly 47 percent of the sun's light energy passes though the atmosphere to heat the land and oceans. In passing through, the atmosphere is warmed by the sun during the day. About one-third of the sun's heat energy goes into the air and the rest heats the land masses and oceans. The warm air, land, and oceans give up their acquired warmth by, ironically, radiating the heat back into space as long wave radiation when half of the planet cools in the darkness of night. We feel this heat flow in the atmosphere with the daily and seasonal variations in temperature. Instead of formulas and meaningless large numbers and strange units of energy, I like to think in more familiar terms. For sure, everyone has felt the sun's heat in many small and curious ways, such as getting into a car in summer or walking barefoot on an asphalt pavement at noon.

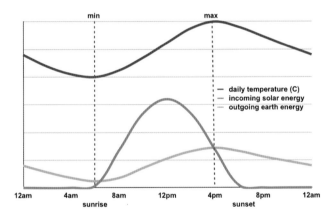

Solar energy flow and daily temperature

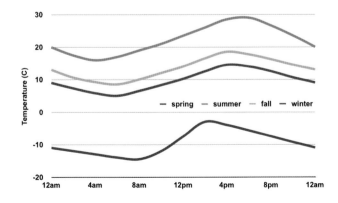

Seasonal variations in daily temperature

On a much larger scale, we can begin to grasp the magnitude of this power. Regardless of where we live on the planet, we experience both a daily and a seasonal change in the temperature as the earth rotates on its axis and orbits the sun. Although it may vary by location and we may find extreme cases of variation, the change in temperature between day and night may typically be in the range of 18 to 28 degrees Fahrenheit halfway between the equator and North Pole. The seasonal variation in temperature caused by the changing angle of the sun's rays as the earth orbits the sun would typically vary at these same latitudes by 50 to 65 degrees Fahrenheit. In Michigan, the variation is from 83 degrees Fahrenheit in the summer to 14 degrees Fahrenheit in the winter - a change of 69 degrees Fahrenheit. Of course these numbers vary somewhat around the world but we can begin to understand the magnitude of this energy if the sun heats half the earth's atmosphere by 25 degrees Fahrenheit over a period of 12 hours. Can you imagine how many matches you would have to light or how many hair dryers you would have to turn on to raise the temperature of the atmosphere to accomplish this much? I can't imagine it by these or any other measure except to say the amount of energy is huge. This becomes even more apparent if you examine the other forms of permanent solar energy - water, wind, and plants.

About 23 percent of the sun's energy drives the water cycle on our planet. This includes the energy needed to convert solid ice to liquid to gaseous water vapor and the raising of water from the surface to the clouds above. Again, can we imagine how many tea kettles would be required if we scooped up the snow from a major winter blizzard and heated it to boiling. Again, the only response is that the amount of energy is huge. To change states and lift this amount of water several hundred and even thousands of feet and distribute it as rain and snow across the land masses is hard to grasp. The potential energy to be released as water follows its destiny to a common lower level has provided energy around the world and throughout recorded history.

A much smaller percentage of the sun's light energy drives the wind, waves, convection, and currents on our planet. Variations in the rate of solar heat absorption between land and sea, high and low altitudes, deep and shallow waters, and light and dark land masses give birth to wind and water flow in a very predictable manner on a long term basis. The mass of air and water in motion represents an impressive energy source by any measure — the magnitude of the energy can be witnessed in the destructive power of extreme natural weather events. More frequently, gentler breezes distribute kinetic energy over the entire surface of the earth, both day and night.

The natural flow from the equator to poles is broken into regions by the rotation of the earth. The regions include the equatorial doldrums, easterly trade winds, horse latitudes, westerlies (which are the primary winds in the United States), and finally the polar easterlies. On a regional basis there are several influences on the strength of the winds. Regardless

However, the result is all of the yearly plant growth encompassing both the new growth of annuals from seed to mature plant and all of the incremental growth of perennial plants and trees on land. To get a feeling of this photosynthetic energy, consider driving past a barren farm field of several hundred acres in March while the winter snow melts surrounded by leafless trees. Return a few months later in late July and walk along row after row of corn growing well above your head and surrounded by the shady canopy of the trees. It is a great deal of energy by any measure.

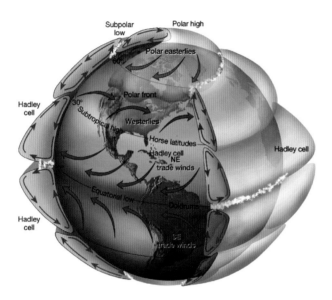

A NASA image depicting the thermal and rotation influences on the earth's wind patterns

of the influences, average annual wind speeds, which are a measure of the energy in the wind, vary from extreme calm to frequently quite strong. Moderate to strong winds are available over a large percentage of the earth's land masses and seas for that matter. Like water power, humanity has found significant uses for this energy throughout recorded history.

On average, less than 1 percent of the sun's light energy goes into photosynthesis. This small fraction of light energy is converted by plant life from water and carbon dioxide in the atmosphere into carbohydrates and oxygen, which are essential to life. About two-thirds of the photosynthetic conversion of the sun's energy occurs on land, while the remaining one-third occurs in the seas. Since photosynthesis relies on only 45 percent of the frequencies in the light's energy, it is not very efficient - a few percent at best. In most cases, it only occurs during the growing months of late spring and summer, which alternate between the Northern and Southern hemisphere. The net effect is that only a small percentage of the sun's energy is actually converted by photosynthesis.

When we add up these huge numbers, the sum is equal to 15,000 times that of our present global energy consumption. While it may be true that we are not able to capture and use all of the sun's energy, it should be clear that one 15 thousandth of that would not be too difficult and may in fact make overwhelming sense considering the alternatives.

Fossil fuels, oil, gas, and coal, are categorized as "temporary" when we understand how they came to be. About 542 million years ago, life forms from simple to very complex began to appear in the shallow seas. In a relatively short period, an abundance of new life forms emerged in what would become known as the Cambrian Explosion. This would continue for over 125 million years before life migrated onto land. This migration was enabled by the formation of the protective ozone layer from the oxygen released by photosynthesis in the seas. During the ensuing Carboniferous Era, life on land flourished, first in the form of plants and then by a vast diversity of animal life. Life on the planet continued in the shallow seas and on land until a cataclysmic event occurred. About

250 million years ago, the Permian-Triassic Extinction resulted in the disappearance and extinction of 96 percent of all marine species and 70 percent of land organisms.

The oil and gas we use today formed in the shallow seas for more than 140 million years after the Cambrian explosion and throughout the Carboniferous Era. The coal we use formed during the Carboniferous Period. Fossil fuels are solar light energy transformed by plant photosynthesis - by far the least of the permanent solar energy forms - with

For combustion, the problem is simple in that both the electrolysis of water and the chemical means of disassociating the hydrogen from the oxygen and carbon consume more energy than is available in recombining them in the combustion process. For example, if you took a small amount of water and put in a 100 units of energy by electrolysis to break up the hydrogen and oxygen atoms and then burned them you would get back far less than the 100 units of energy. Likewise, separating hydrogen from carbon by steam reformation yields the same results in that it

Annual and perennial plant growth from solar photosynthesis

the aid of the food chain. It is stored in the earth under pressure to form oil and gas in the shallow seas and coal seams on the land masses. It is temporary because when it's gone, it's really gone.

Nearly 4 billion years ago, 90 percent of the earth's surface was covered by water. As the continents emerged, the oceans would be reduced to 71 percent of the earth's surface. The seawater in the oceans is made up of about 97 percent water, or hydrogen and oxygen. On a mass basis, seawater is nearly 86 percent oxygen and 11 percent hydrogen. Hydrogen is the lightest element and most abundant in the universe, making up 75 percent of the elemental mass. Hydrogen is therefore an enticing source of energy. Hydrogen reacts readily with the oxygen in air to release thermal energy and yield water, a clean combustion product. Hydrogen also fuels the fusion energy process of the sun and thus is looked at as a fuel for fusion energy on earth. Pure hydrogen gas is very rare on earth due in part to its lightness but mostly because of its affinity to uniting with oxygen and carbon. Thus hydrogen is normally found combined with oxygen and carbon, two very abundant elements, in the form of water and hydrocarbons. Using hydrogen as an energy source is problematic.

takes more energy than it yields, and a great deal of greenhouse gases are the byproduct. Until a process is found that overcomes these problems, hydrogen as a combustion fuel will inevitably remain illusive.

The other proposal for hydrogen involves converting it into helium using the same process that powers the sun. Known as fusion energy, the "fusing" of two hydrogen molecules into a single helium molecule yields a tremendous amount of heat energy from the resultant loss of a small amount of mass. Although the prospects are enormous, the technological barriers to achieve this remain overwhelming in the near term. Regardless, the effort to make progress towards overcoming these barriers is by definition large in scope, requiring cooperation, and technical and financial resources of global proportions.

Practically speaking, it is illogical to convert water or methane to hydrogen and burn it. It would make more sense to take the energy that would be required and use it directly. In the case of fusion, it is not possible to light a single light bulb today and it is not clear whether it will ever be possible even if it made sense to try. If you look up in a clear daytime sky there is a fusion reactor of immense and enduring capacity that is ready to continue to serve us.

The crust of our planet is a cornucopia of elements in large amounts. The crust varies in thickness over a general range of three to six miles beneath the oceans to 20 to 30 miles at the land masses. The potential energy when you exclude the solar based fossil fuels is somewhat limited however. On a planetary basis the earth is made up of 32 percent iron, 30 percent oxygen, 15 percent silicon, 14 percent magnesium, 3 percent sulfur, 2 percent nickel, 1.5 percent each of calcium and aluminum, and a little over 1 percent of everything else. The crust of

our lives. The elements can also provide high value energy storage in the form of rechargeable batteries in both independent and grid connected electrical systems. Secondary cells can play a pivotal role in enabling both solar and wind energy use around the world. In addition to reliability, another great attribute of rechargeable batteries is that they are also highly recyclable and reusable.

Another source of energy from the earth's crust can be derived from nuclear fission, or the splitting of atoms to release heat energy from the resulting loss

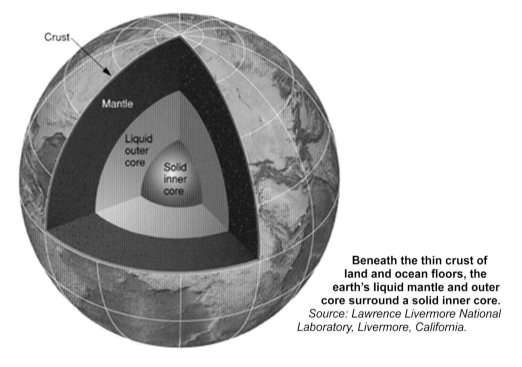

Beneath the thin crust of land and ocean floors, the earth's liquid mantle and outer core surround a solid inner core.
Source: Lawrence Livermore National Laboratory, Livermore, California.

the earth in the form of rocks is nearly all oxides of these elements: silica (59.7 percent), alumina (15.4 percent), lime (4.9 percent), magnesia (4.3 percent), sodium oxide (3.5 percent), iron (II) oxide (3.5 percent), potassium oxide (2.8 percent), iron (III) oxide (2.6 percent), water (1.5 percent), titanium oxide (0.65 percent), and phosphorus oxide (0.2 percent), which leaves 0.8 percent for all the other elements in the periodic table. The potential of this source in the form of chemical energy is relatively minor in quantity but very large in terms of quality. Certainly, the elements play an important role in storing and moving energy to where it is needed. The chemical energy used for primary and secondary batteries that power small high quality portable electrical devices, such as music players, GPS, flashlights, cell phones, cars, toys, instruments, and much more, is an invaluable contributor to the role of electricity in

of mass. When a uranium atom is split, the loss of a small amount of mass will release a large amount of heat energy. Uranium is the heaviest naturally occurring element and is found everywhere in rock and even seawater in very small concentrations. Extracting and processing uranium for use is very energy intensive which practically limits the feasibility of mining to where the concentration levels are quite high. Estimates on the potential contribution of nuclear fission in the early years were predicated on the promise of advanced technology that neither came to be nor is even considered viable anymore. The potential energy contribution of uranium in the absence of other technology breakthroughs is limited to a few hundred years at best. The largest world estimated reserves are located in Australia (30 percent), Kazakhstan (17 percent), and Canada (12 percent). Present day production is led by Canada (28 percent) and Australia (23 percent), with Kazakhstan, Russia, Niger, Namibia, and Uzbekistan making up the bulk of the balance. The United States reserves are low concentration and thus poor in quality resulting in a global production of 4 percent. Europe, with significant nuclear generation, produces less than 3 percent of what it uses. Although nuclear power eliminates gaseous emissions, it is burdened by the responsibility of long-term management of its deadly spent radioactive fuel. Regardless of the merits of this source of energy, it is excessively expensive to split atoms to boil water and produce electricity, and reactor sales have fallen despite massive financial support from nations everywhere.

Beneath the crust lies the mantel and outer and inner core of the earth. Standing on the surface on a cool winter day it is easy to overlook that a few miles beneath our feet lies the molten rock center of our planet which is several thousand degrees Fahrenheit in temperature. The mantel is about 1,800 miles thick and represents about 70 percent of the earth's volume. The temperature of the mantel is about 1,600 degrees Fahrenheit near the crust and about 8,000 degrees Fahrenheit at the core boundary. The iron-rich core extends 1,350 miles from the center to where the mantel begins and makes up the balance of 30 percent of the earth's volume. The outer core is liquid and the inner core is solid with temperatures ranging from 8,000 to 12,500 degrees Fahrenheit. The amount of heat energy in the earth – geothermal – is significant but getting to it on a broad scale represents significant challenges. Where the mantel is close to the surface, geothermal energy can be quite advantageous and has proven successful in many cases. Iceland, which lies on the Mid-Atlantic Ridge, is the most notable example. The island country generates 99 percent of its electricity from geothermal.

Born from a massive collision with our sister planet Theia nearly 4.5 billion years ago, the moon has been stabilizing earth's climate and atmosphere through its gravitation ever since. The moon provides the force that holds our axis of rotation steady to allow an environment essential for life to exist, a unique circumstance in the universe. Although it may also not be obvious, the moon's gravity is a force that provides significant energy input on a continuous basis to our planet. It lifts the oceans on the near side of the earth and lowers them on the far side in what we know as the tides. The amount of potential energy in the tides is significant, as lifting the entire weight of the water in the oceans several feet a day is no small task. Capturing the water at high tide and controlling the flow through a turbine in a manner similar to a dam as it returns to low tide has been proposed as a means to harness this energy. A serious proposal to harness 1,000 megawatts of tidal power from the Passamaquoddy-Cobscook Bay archipelago, located at the entrance to the Bay of Fundy in Maine where the mean tidal range is over 18 feet, was developed between 1912 and 1935 but never got off the drawing board.

Additionally, kinetic tidal energy as the flowing water advances and recedes has been proposed as a means of producing electricity using underwater turbines. Interestingly, the U. S. Coast Guard recently announced plans to test underwater turbines in Passamaquoddy-Cobscook Bay. Although there may be limits to the contribution of tidal energy, it could be significant in selected local or regional areas. Regardless, it will be considered and looked to in the future as a possible contributor to a diversified energy mix. Tidal power projects that harness both the kinetic and potential energy of the tides should be developed. As a point of interest, it should be noted that the gravitational pull of the moon is getting smaller as it moves about 1.5 inches farther away from the earth each year. Not to worry, though, since its influence will be around for quite a while.

From the sun, earth, and moon, the energy forms are converted into energy mediums by various means from combustion to machines of all sorts, such as engines, turbines, and generators. The energy mediums, namely heat, mechanical, electrical, chemical, and material, can be used directly or converted by yet another machine to another medium or for a desired use or final product. The energy in coal, for example, is released as heat by combustion to boil water and create steam to turn a turbine to produce mechanical energy which in turn drives a generator to produce electricity that flows through wires to be converted to perform work, satisfy needs, or fulfill wants. Of all the mediums, electricity is the most interesting to me because it is the most general. All of the energy sources can be converted to electricity and converted again to accomplish a myriad of work, wants, and needs by a limitless array of devices.

So let's rejoin the founding fathers with our knowledge of energy and see how things developed into where they are today.

Chapter 2

DISCOVERY *and* UNDERSTANDING

James Watt's efficient double acting steam engine launches the industrial revolution.
Source: http://darkwing. uoregon.edu/~klio/ sci/18thCentury.htm.

Let's go back to the summer of 1776. We find the founding fathers living in harmony with nature - plant and animal biofuels, horses, and sail power. A few events are worth noting to add a little perspective. A year ago in 1775, Scottish inventor James Watt designed a new and improved steam engine that used 75 percent less coal than the Newcomen steam engine that was first demonstrated 64 years earlier, in 1712.

The engine burned coal to produce steam, which drove a mechanical device that would power industrial equipment. Watt's new steam engine design would dramatically accelerate the pace of the fledgling industrial revolution.

Given our understanding of energy sources, it is worthwhile to note that the first coal mine in the United States began shipping coal in 1730, but it would be another 120 years before coal use surpassed wood. Thomas Jefferson in a few years would switch to coal to heat the White House. It would be nearly 40 years until the first natural gas well was drilled by William Hart in 1821 in Fredonia, New York. The first oil well would be drilled in Titusville, Pennsylvania in 1859, yielding 2,000 barrels in its first year.

The development and growth of electricity was facilitated by the development and growth of steam power which preceded it by about 20 years

and developed along a parallel path until merging fortunes 100 years later. So let us start with the early beginnings of our understanding of electricity. As noted earlier, and despite Benjamin Franklin's bold tinkering, our understanding of electricity was confined primarily to the atmospheric phenomena of lightening, curiosity with static discharge, and the rare but strange magnetic attraction. Our electrical instruments were amber stones that became electrically charged when rubbed vigorously with cloth and the pull of lodestone magnets. In 1893 that would begin to change dramatically by an unlikely chain of events.

The earliest steps began in the laboratory of Luigi Galvani, a professor of anatomy and natural science in Bologna, Italy. He was dissecting a frog on a brass table with an iron knife when a nerve bundle in the dead frog's leg was touched and the leg contracted. From his experience with Leyden jars and knowledge of the effects of sparks, he concluded there was electricity in the frog. He convinced a few colleagues to embrace his animal electricity theory.

His friend and fellow natural scientist, Allesandro Volta, was skeptical and thought the electricity was in the metal and not the frog. He correctly concludes that the frog, thankfully, was actually a poor conductor between two dissimilar metals where electrons

Luigi Galvani's experiments lead to his theory of "electric fluid" as a "life force," as illustrated in the book, *De Viribus Electricitatis in Motu Musculari Commentarius*, **in 1791**.

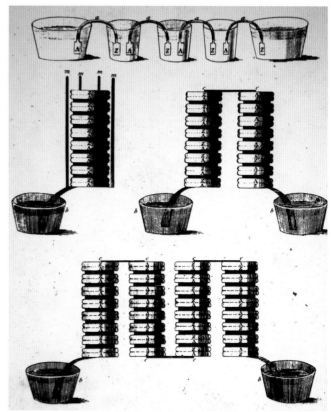

In the 1800 *Philosophical Transactions of the Royal Society of London*, **Allesandro Volta redefines the "primary" electrochemical cell with his "crown of cups" and "voltaic pile" batteries.**

were migrating because of their atomic structure and associated electrical characteristics. To make his point he developed the "Crown of cups" and the "Voltaic pile," a stack with several layers of silver, moistened paper, and zinc, and demonstrated that the effects could be increased by making larger layers and more layers. The Voltaic pile is the first primary electrochemical cell and served as the basis for the ubiquitous disposable, or more correctly recyclable, battery.

The battery evolved over the next 200 years from the largest primary source of electricity for research purposes to the smallest and very specialized source we know today. However, for the next 25 to 75 years, the electrochemical cell stayed primarily in university and private laboratories for study and to provide a deeper understanding of electricity by being the primary source of electrical current flowing in conductors. During this period, leading scientists around the world changed the materials and molded them into every possible shape, size, and configuration to gain a richer understanding. Today, the primary electrochemical cells have become small electricity sources to power our flashlights, portable radios, watches, hearing aids, toys, garage door openers, television remotes, cameras, and numerous other

This illustration from *Geschichte der Telegraphie,* 1905, **shows a plunge battery using Wollaston U-shaped electrodes, which is one of many forms taken on by the battery**.

As depicted in A. Niaudet's book *Electric Batteries* **in 1880, a laboratory battery of Daniell cells would lead to commercialization for the early telecommunication industry.**

familiar items. We see them at checkout counters of grocery, pharmacy, convenience, hardware, and department stores everywhere.

Although the primary battery is an important part of modern electricity, it is in terms of quantity a very small portion of our power usage. It did, however, serve as a vehicle in understanding electricity in the early years and thus for the next great advancement in the science of electricity - electromagnetism. A significant majority of electrical technology is based on the interaction of electricity flowing in a wire conductor around an iron core to create a magnet and produce a mechanical force. And conversely, a mechanical force moving a conductor in the presence of a magnet creates the flow of electricity in the conductor. These simple concepts from their earliest knowledge would lead to the discovery of the second major electrical device - the "dynamo." The dynamo is a rotating device that converts mechanical energy to electrical energy and vice versa. It would become known today by its two variants, the electric generator and electric motor. And like the primary cell, the earliest indications of the basic relationship came from the most simple of origins. A physics professor at Copenhagen, Hans Oersted, noted in 1820 that a compass needle

would reorient itself when electric current, from a primary cell, was flowing in a nearby wire.

This simple experiment would send scientists whose names are familiar to electrical terminology, namely André-Marie Ampère, Joseph Henry, and Michael Faraday, into experiments and proposals for designs of an equally amazing variety to the study undertaken with the electrochemical cell. The myriad of experiments and devices emanating from this scientific curiosity of electromagnetism went on for the next several decades. The net result shown is this simple example in the illustration below. When the handle is turned and electrons flow in the wire, you have an electric "generator." When the wires are connected to a battery and the handle turns, you have an electric "motor." Connect it to a steam engine, or any other mechanical source, and electricity flows as long as the steam engine turns the generator.

At this point in history, nearly all of the work involved direct current electricity where the electrons always flow in the same direction. This was primarily due to all the work and understanding that had been facilitated by the electrochemical primary cell, which was a direct current device. In order to accomplish this with a rotating generator, the output wires had

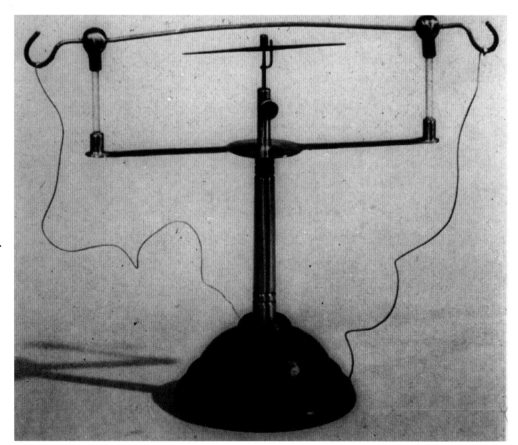

Shown in this USNM Smithsonian photo is a model of Oersted's 1820 wire experiment.

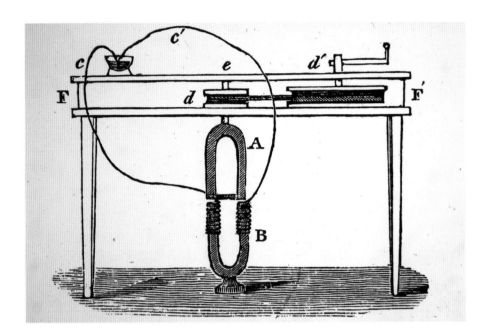

The *American Journal of Science* of April 1883 demonstrates how Hippolyte Pixii's magneto generator converts mechanical energy to electricity in a laboratory demonstration by A. M. Ampère in 1832.

William Sturgeon's *Annals of Electricity*, 1840, illustrates Joule's motor and how it converts electricity to mechanical energy.

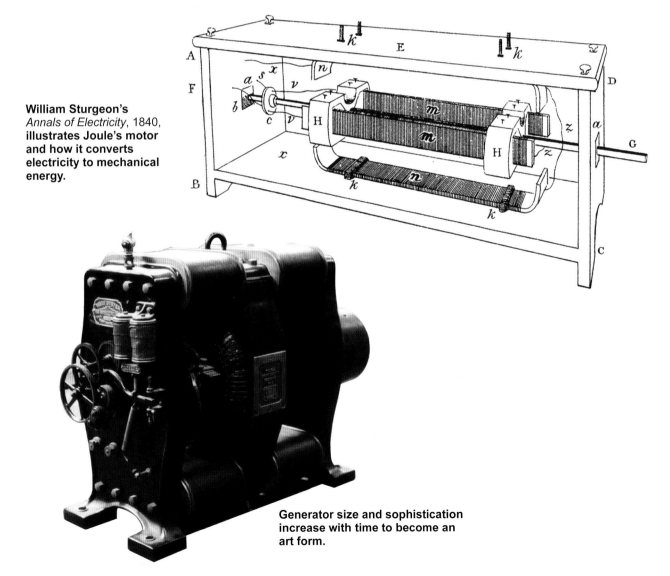

Generator size and sophistication increase with time to become an art form.

to be switched or "commutated" as the generator turned to preclude the electrons from reversing their direction of flow. This was accomplished by "brushes" positioned around the "armature" where the rotating wires come together. Later on, the direct-current generator would be turned into an alternating current generator by eliminating the brushes, which would wear out, and develop equipment to allow and accommodate electrons flowing in both directions.

Today, the generator is virtually the sole source of all the electricity that we use. Its sibling technology, the electric motor, consumes a large percentage of the electricity that the generators produce in the familiar form of refrigerators, washers, dryers, furnaces, air conditioners, fans, blenders, etc. in homes and in powering most commercial and industrial equipment

The early discoveries by Oersted would, however, lead to electricity as a power medium when used with rotating machinery. Watt's steam engine and the electric generator fortunes merged at this point and became very popular in the coming decades. The same electromagnetic principles, when used with linear machinery, would serve as the foundation for electricity as a communication medium - telegraph, telephone, and internet. Batteries would also play a major role in telecommunications technology development to this day.

The availability of two sources of electricity, namely the electrochemical primary cell and dynamo, or "generator" as we will refer to it from here on, contributed to a continuing quest for more knowledge about this fascinating phenomenon. In 1859, 66 years after Galvani's discoveries, French scientist Gaston Planté through his work came to the realization that the discharge process of an electrochemical cell could be reversed and thus the "secondary" electrochemical cell or "rechargeable" battery was discovered. In my opinion it becomes the third of the five basic building blocks of electricity. The impact of this device is that energy can be "stored" chemically, withdrawn on demand, and replaced when convenient by another battery, generator, or other source.

The effect we see today is that the rechargeable battery gives us electric mobility. It is a mainstay of transportation as it starts and powers our cars and trucks, allows us to carry our telecommunications system in a purse or pocket phone, and lets us operate power tools anywhere without being plugged in. The rechargeable battery provides continuity in an emergency when power is lost, including safety lighting in buildings, protection for computers and other

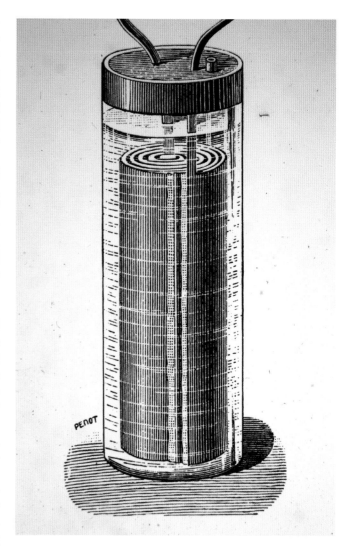

As illustrated in the book *Recherches sur l'electricité,* 1883, **Gaston Planté discovers the "secondary" electrochemical cell, or rechargeable storage battery.**

sensitive equipment, and back-up power for a variety of common devices. It would become a fundamental element in the use of solar, wind, and a broad range of energy sources and has many desirable performance qualities as we will see.

With the understanding of electricity growing with each new development, devices were now ready to move from the laboratories to public demonstration and practical uses in the ensuing years. During the early use of electricity, small projects began to find a variety of special uses that would come into being with a constant flow of ideas about using this new force. The prominent proponents would leave their mark as business icons and dominate the broad-scale use of electricity in the distant future, such as Thomas Edison and J. P. Morgan in the form of

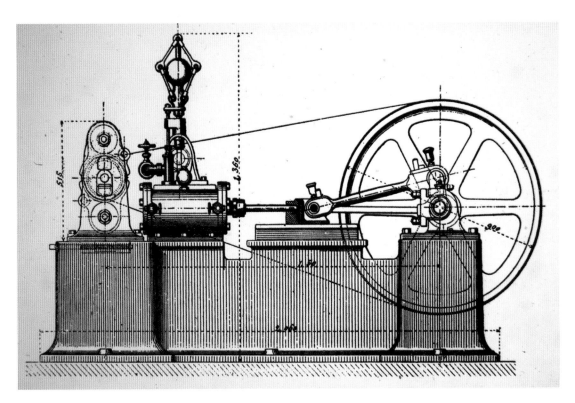

The generator and steam engine, as explored in the 1877 journal Revue industrielle, unite, merging their fortunes forevermore.

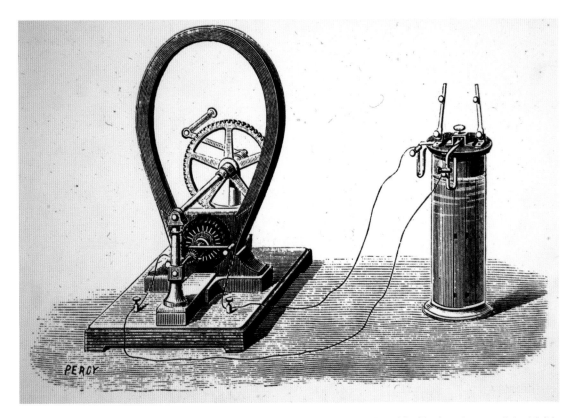

Charging a Planté cell with a Gramme magneto generator, as depicted in *Recherches sur l'electricité* in 1883.

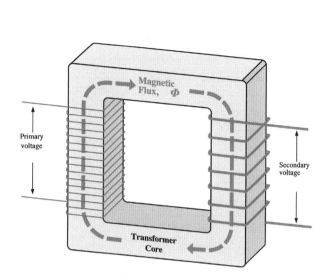

A transformer raises or lowers the alternating current voltage from primary to secondary in proportion to the ratio of the number of turns of wire.

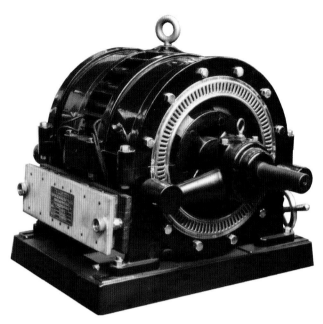

An alternating current generator, alternator, is used with the transformer.

General Electric, and George Westinghouse. The person most responsible for the electric supply network of today, however, was the Serbian scientist Nikola Tesla. The relatively little known Tesla, an eccentric and driven engineer and inventor who died destitute in 1943, had perhaps the largest impact of any single person on today's alternating current electric supply system, as well as a host of other major contributions for related electric technology. The device that dramatically changed the electric system was the alternating current transformer, which was a simple device with no moving parts. A transformer could increase the voltage from a generator to allow it to be "transmitted" efficiently over long distances where it could be decreased to a lower value first at a substation transformer and distributed over shorter distances and then lowered again using a small service transformer to allow it to be used at a final lower voltage level in homes, commerce, and industry. The transformer would require a compatible alternating current generator, or alternator, that would eliminate the commutator brushes, and operate at higher voltages

This simple device served as a basis for the "economy of scale" argument that led to an advantage of alternating current over direct current systems. A similar device did not exist for direct current which limited the size of a power plant and the area that each electric power plant could serve. In the figure below we can see that it would take nine small direct current power plants distributed equally to serve a given area. By contrast, a single large alternating current power plant using a high voltage transmission

and distribution network of transformers could serve the same area. It was more economical to build one large power plant with transformers rather than several small power plants. The large power plant could be located far from the area being served to move the noise and exhaust farther away. The large power plant could also be located conveniently closer to a large source of cooling water needed to condense the steam from the turbine.

The whole debate over direct current versus alternating current was a very public, high-profile debate that went on between powerful interests lined up in support of the primary debaters - Edison on the side of direct current and industrialist Westinghouse who wound up holding important elements of Tesla's alternating current patents. Edison correctly argued that direct current was safer than alternating current. Westinghouse effectively ended the debate when he received the award to build the alternating current generating plant powered by Niagara Falls to send electricity 20 miles to the city of Buffalo, New York. A feat that Edison's direct current system simply could not do. Edison would team up with J.P. Morgan to establish the General Electric Co. and ultimately converted to alternating current technology.

By 1893, 100 years since Galvani's experiments, all the pieces were in place for the electric supply system to grow to its position of dominance, or perhaps over dominance, as I will demonstrate in our electricity system of today.

Unfortunately, the last and most significant piece of electrical technology, especially for the future, would not be discovered for another 61 years, and

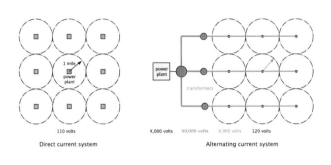

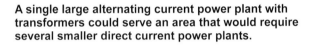

| Direct current system | Alternating current system |

A single large alternating current power plant with transformers could serve an area that would require several smaller direct current power plants.

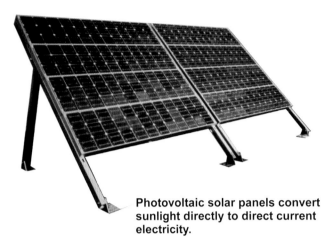

Photovoltaic solar panels convert sunlight directly to direct current electricity.

An early transformer substation raises the voltage from 11,000 to 22,000.

well after our national supply network had been sufficiently established. In 1901, Tesla proposed converting radiant energy directly to electricity, including radiant solar energy, but did little to develop the concept. Despite earlier small scale developments over the years, the coming age of solar electricity only began in 1954 when researchers at Bell Laboratories found that silicon doped with impurities was very sensitive to light. The resulting photovoltaic cell converted the sun's light energy directly to electricity at reasonable efficiencies. I wish that I could make the photovoltaic cell more complicated in scientific terms but the various proposals all function in the same simple way. The light energy from the sun falling on a solar panel causes electricity to flow in the two wires that are connected to the cells. The promising technology was first used on spacecraft in 1958 and has been an important power source for manned and unmanned spacecraft ever since. On a more down to earth basis, the use of photovoltaic panels has been increasing steadily over the years as the technology advances and becomes more cost effective. It is truly unfortunate that solar cells came along late in the maturation process of our supply network. On the other hand, it is fortunate that this device has come along at all and promises to be the dominant source of electricity in the future.

Chapter 3

Early Applications

A Gramme generator, illustrated in the 1874 *Revue Industrielle*, replaced the battery for silver electroplating.

As noted earlier, it would take about 100 years before the early electrochemical discoveries of Italians Luigi Galvani and Alessandro Volta combined with the understanding of electromagnetism through the contributions of Hans Christian Oerstad, Michael Faraday, André-Marie Ampère, and others, became commercialized and began to have a rapidly increasing influence on everyday life. The early years of scientific inquiry into electric principles and devices were confined to university and private laboratory experimentation. A few early uses were discovered, and the science of electricity branched into two distinct technologies - communication and power – which developed slowly along parallel paths at different rates. As time went by, machinists and engineers made improvements in generating equipment and electrical devices at the same time that new and improved uses for electricity were being developed. At the turn of the century, the electrification of America began in earnest and has not let up since - new, better, faster, more.

When Volta first discovered the "voltaic pile," he had several made and gave them to his friends and university associates. One of these associates was Luigi Brugnatelli, a chemistry professor, who used the voltaic pile to develop the electro-deposition process to electroplate gold on a silver object in 1805. By the 1840s, other scientists expanded the electroplating process to include bright nickel, brass, tin, and zinc using batteries. Early direct current generators driven by water power or steam engines supplanted the batteries which had to be constantly replaced as they became discharged. Electroplating provided many benefits. In addition to a smooth hard finish, it resulted in improved corrosion and abrasion resistance. The real accelerator came with silver-plating - "The Age of Cheap." Everything that could be silver plated was, such as flatware, tea sets, candlestick holders, hairbrushes, and snuff boxes, and the demand was great.

The long road to commercialization of telecommunications is a subject equal to and perhaps larger in scope than the progress of power and is worth an in-depth analysis unto itself. For our purposes, we will limit our inquiry to the early years and shared experiences with electric power development. At first, the telecommunications pathway - telegraph, telephone, radio, television, cable, satellite, and Internet - seemed to develop faster than the power pathway. The concept of transmitting a "signal" over a distance by wire had scientists such as Carl Friedrich Gauss, Joseph Henry, Wilhelm Weber and Samuel Morse in hot pursuit of a workable solution.

Samuel Morse's telegraph signals the beginning of the age of communication.

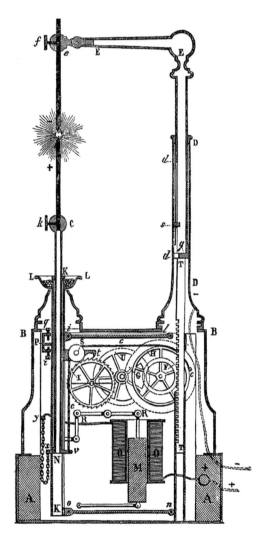

A version of Victor Serrin's arc-light regulator as depicted in T. du Moncel's *Exposé des applications de l'electricité* **in 1856**

In America, Morse started thinking about an electric "telegraph" aboard ship on return from a visit to France. A few years later, he became a professor of arts and design at New York University and found time to work on his telegraph ideas. With the help of Leonard Gale, a chemistry professor and friend, they were able to transmit a signal 10 miles by the end of 1837. Alfred Vail heard of Morse's work and agreed to build a system based on the design and help with patents. A few years later with the addition of the "key" and the "code," they received a $30,000 federal grant and set up a successful demonstration of the telegraph along 40 miles of railroad lines between Baltimore and Washington. In 1845, Morse went private with the Magnetic Telegraph Co. His early success created a host of competitors - some fleeting but also some enduring, like the Associated Press and Western Union - and the information age was off and running.

From the earliest experiments, researchers noticed the phenomenon of "arcing," a spark flowing through the air that was visible, when connecting or disconnecting batteries or switching circuits on or off. At this point, scientists began thinking about how to use the "arc" to produce large amounts of "light" to be able to see at night and in dimly lit places. Of course, the arc-light was the first product in pursuit of this capability. This would be a more challenging task than anticipated because the temperature of an electric arc is extremely high (several thousand degrees Fahrenheit) and has a tendency to melt or vaporize surrounding materials including the electrodes that create the arc. The result is that most arc lamps were large and very complicated, not to mention intensely bright and noisy.

Work went on and several different lamps were produced and primarily used for highly publicized exhibition and demonstration projects. The first being the feat of Louis Deleuil to demonstrate an arc light at the Place de la Concorde in Paris in 1843 using 200 Bunsen cells and carbon electrodes. It was simply not practical for a long period of time as the Bunsen cells would discharge and have to be replaced. The next demonstration was powered by a new alternating current generator, or alternator, to supply 62 lights, rated 300 to 500 equivalent candles each, to light the Avenue de la Opera and Place de la Opera in Paris in 1878, and the "City of Lights" was born.

This demonstration set the world abuzz to street lighting, or "illuminating," and the days were about to get longer. The arc light found its way to demonstrations in a lighthouse at Cap de la Hève and even

Cartoonist's image in the 1848 *L'Illustration* of a concierge
giving a hotel guest an electric arc "candle"

The Avenue de la Opera in Paris (illustrated in the 1881 *La Luminaire electrique*)
is illuminated by the equivalent of 25,000 candles in 1878.

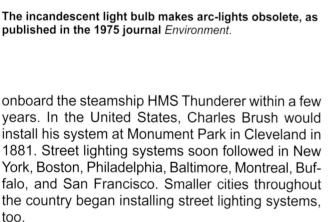

The incandescent light bulb makes arc-lights obsolete, as published in the 1975 journal *Environment.*

Electric "traction," or trolleys, would replace horsepower with kilowatt-hours in cities across America.

onboard the steamship HMS Thunderer within a few years. In the United States, Charles Brush would install his system at Monument Park in Cleveland in 1881. Street lighting systems soon followed in New York, Boston, Philadelphia, Baltimore, Montreal, Buffalo, and San Francisco. Smaller cities throughout the country began installing street lighting systems, too.

Despite the great advances of Paul Jablochkoff and other early successes, the arc light was not to be. At about this same time, Sir Joseph Swan in Britain and, about a year later, Thomas Edison in the United States were moving lighting in a new direction using a filament that "incandesces" in a glass bulb with the air evacuated. Smaller, cheaper, better light, and much longer life made a huge difference. At first Swan and Edison formed a company together, known as the Edison and Swan Electric Light Co., or "Ediswan," to produce lamps of Swan's design. Later Edison went

his own way with General Electric. The incandescent lamp made the light bulb suitable for indoor use in stores and homes and drove further innovation.

It is human nature to put wheels under every new invention and electricity is no different in this respect. With electric wires everywhere along main thoroughfares, horsepower would be replaced by kilowatt hours. The first schemes for propelling large vehicles along tracks to carry people to their jobs started as soon as generators and motors became commercially available. Some of these transportation devices relied on electric power beneath them in the tracks, while others relied on overhead conductors. An early trolley or "traction" system began operating in Richmond, Virginia, in 1888. Boston would soon follow. In 1892, the Detroit Citizens Street Railway began operating street car lines on Jefferson and Mack Avenues with routes planned along Woodward, Grand River, and Michigan Avenue, which all radiated from the city

Electric trolleys would evolve into mass public transit and interurban trains.

center. Just before the turn of the century, New York City embarked on an ambitious plan to move its public rail system underground and electrify it, becoming the subway system that would be the envy of every American city in the future. Electric trains would come to dominate the passenger rail networks around urban areas and are the mainstay of systems around Chicago, Los Angeles, and the entire Northeast corridor from the District of Columbia to Boston. Many freight rails also rely on electric power.

With electric lines providing public street illumination and traction lines moving through many cities and towns, it wasn't long before power lines would be offered to businesses along the avenues and to homeowners down the adjoining streets. The electrification process was indeed off and running.

The fascination with flameless electric lamps propelled electric technology towards rapid commercialization. A variety of designers and manufacturers produced generators that were coupled with every known source of mechanical power, namely steam engines and water turbines at the time. The steam turbine, Otto four-stroke, and diesel-cycle engines were still in their infancy, but they would ultimately be connected to a generator, too.

In Grand Rapids, Michigan, the Wolverine Chair Co. installed a small hydro electric plant on the Grand River to power 16 arc lights in its factory in 1880. In 1882, the Appleton Edison Light Co., in Appleton, Wisconsin, started producing electricity with the nation's first hydroelectric power plant. The company harnessed the potential energy of the Fox River to supply 12.5 kilowatts of electricity for lighting and to power two buildings and the home of the paper mill's owner. By 1886, nearly 50 hydropower plants were in operation or under construction, and by 1889, there were over 200 electric companies listed as providers of hydroelectric power.

On an even grander scale, the power plant at Niagara Falls began supplying power to the city of Buffalo in 1895. It would suffer a catastrophic collapse in 1956. By 1900, water power was producing 40 percent of the electricity in the United States. The Trade Dollar Mining Co. built a hydroelectric plant that began operation in 1901 at Swan Falls on the Snake River in Idaho.

The Blake Snake mine was fully electrified with compressor motors for drilling, lighting, and a rail system for miners and mineral lift. This mining operation not only produced its own power but made the excess available to the surrounding community of Silver City. When the mine closed, the dam became the center of development for the regional electric provider that would become Idaho Power. There are hundreds of stories like this one where cities, towns, and industries put the energy of water to work via the medium of electricity.

The federal government would take control of the national waterways through the passage of the Federal Water Power Act of 1902. This led to the formation of the Bureau of Land Reclamation and the federal dominance in hydroelectric power development and thus to becoming a producer of electricity. The Roosevelt Dam and Salt River Project were the first major dams and soon were followed by Muscle Shoals, Boulder/Hoover, Grand Coulee, the Tennessee Valley Authority, Bonneville Power Administration, and others. Today, about 10 percent of our electricity is provided by hydro-power primarily from these public entities.

At the same time generators were connected to steam engines in record numbers and used for all kinds of work, needs, and wants, both private and public. Many office and retail buildings had steam boilers for heating. Adding a steam engine connected to a generator in the steam line provided electricity for "incandescent" lighting and other purposes and became an immediate hit.

One of those other purposes for early electric power generation was to lift elevators. My grandfather, Wilhelm August Toepfer, started his career as a young man by operating the first elevator in downtown Detroit at the Moffett Building to support his new wife and first of seven children. At the time, building heights reached a maximum in the major cities of about 5 to 7 stories. The elevator, in conjunction with steel building techniques, allowed the height of buildings to soar to unimagined heights in the next 25 years. When my grandfather retired, he was the building superintendent of the 654-foot-high, 47-story

Thomas Edison connected a steam engine to his heating system which, with a belt, drove a generator for lights in his Menlo Park, New Jersey, lab.

The Westinghouse alternating current hydroelectric plant at Niagara Falls began operation in 1895 and spelled the beginning of the end for direct current.

Private hydropower drives the generators for the Blake Snake mine in Idaho.

Federal control of the waterways leads to big dam projects for electricity, irrigation, and transportation.

Penobscot building, which was the tallest building in Detroit and the third tallest building in the United States when it opened in 1928.

Diesel engines, gas engines, and steam turbines that were more fuel efficient became available to turn generators and caused electric power usage to soar again with private and municipal systems. The power plants would grow in size as a result, and the steam turbine would come to dominate electrical generation.

Private industry would put power production machinery to work in commercial and industrial factories. When Henry Ford built the renowned Rouge Plant, he installed a massive 345 megawatt power plant to supply his own electricity. In later years, Ford built a series of small hydroelectric powered manufacturing plants in towns in southeast Michigan's watershed to help farmers earn additional money in the winters during the waning years of the Great Depression.

Electric systems even found their way onto moving equipment. To this day, every boat, from small pleasure crafts and luxury yachts to passenger cruise ships and commercial ships, operates its own electric power plant. Likewise, every airplane, train, bus, recreational vehicle, and truck that uses electric power is fitted with its own autonomous electric power plant.

All of these endeavors delighted the investors and financial interests. Their vision of the commercialization of electricity was to manufacture and sell as many pieces of electrical equipment, such as generators, motors, lights, wire, and switches, as they could to any person, company, or public entity that wanted to buy it at a fair price.

Edison, on the other hand, fought for the idea of selling electricity rather than selling equipment. He argued that in highly populated urban areas it would make more sense to have a single large generator to send electricity through wires to all the surrounding businesses and homes rather than each of these businesses running their own small power plant. Fair

A steam engine and a generator connected to steam heating systems produced electricity.

enough for urban areas, but this did not address rural America.

In the years that followed, Edison would be locked in a fierce technical battle with his rival George Westinghouse. Edison ultimately lost. Selling electricity would move forward with the formation of regional electric monopolies from the consolidation of the 1920s - Consolidated Edison in New York, consolidated from 29 separate electric companies, and Commonwealth Edison in Chicago, an empire built on the acquisition of dozens of small power producers by Edison's former secretary Samuel Insull. In a deft move, Insull argued in his "please don't throw me in the briar patch" style for "regulation" knowing full well that legal decisions required regulators to set rates at levels which would allow a fair rate of return for investors. Accordingly, with guaranteed profitability it was in their interest to invest large sums that the capital markets were quite willing to throw at them, allowing them to dominate the markets from other risky investments in the "unregulated" sector.

In the last century, this business model, with additional federal support through the "peaceful" atom program, has given us the private investor-owned central station network that serves the vast majority of homes, businesses, and industry in the United States. No matter who you are or where you live, there is one primary source of electricity – the power company.

The new internal combustion engines would get connected to a generator.

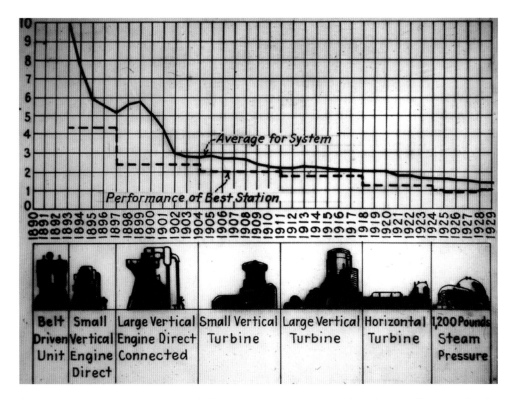

Steam engine advancements and size reduces the amount of coal to produce a unit of electricity.

The horizontal high pressure steam turbine would become the preferred and enduring choice for driving a generator.

Edison started on his quest to sell electricity with the Pearl Street Station in the heart of New York's financial district in 1882, as illustrated in the 1975 journal *Environment*.

Henry Ford built an electric power plant to supply electricity to his renowned
Rouge Plant complex.

Central station generating plants would come to dominate city skylines.

Chapter 4

FARM ELECTRIC PLANTS

Charles F. Kettering.
Courtesy of the Scharchburg Archives, Kettering University, Flint, Michigan.

Despite a virtual explosion in quantity and variety of electrical use in the cities and larger towns, the rest of America, encompassing vast areas of the nation, did not have access to electricity. In 1910, when the population of the United States was 92 million and 54 percent lived in rural areas, electricity was virtually unheard of for farms, cabins, and buildings of any kind that were located far from the cities. Flame lamps, hand pumps for drawing water, and outhouses were the norm. An occasional windmill for the more fortunate would pump water when the wind was blowing. That was all about to change through the genius of American inventor Charles Franklin Kettering.

Kettering, who became affectionately known as "Boss Ket," was a teacher, engineer, scientist, inventor, mentor, businessman, leader, and humanitarian. The impact of his efforts over a life of service, as huge as it was, is not as well known as it should be. This is especially true of his accomplishments to provide electricity to farms and remote places. Born in Ohio in 1876, Kettering, an avid reader who suffered from severe eyestrain, was fascinated by all things electrical. With money he earned from his first job, he bought a telephone and immediately took it apart to understand how it worked. After graduating from Ohio State University with an electrical engineering degree in 1904, he began his career at the National Cash Register Co. where he developed a "breakthrough" electric motor to eliminate the crank handle that was so difficult to operate on cash registers at the time. In 1909, Kettering and business associate Edward Deeds formed the Dayton Engineering Laboratory Co., which became more commonly known as Delco. Their first task was to develop an electric starter for the automobile to eliminate the feared hand crank sticking out of the radiator. In doing so, he developed the basic automobile electric system used in cars, as well as trucks, buses, motorcycles, and virtually every type of vehicle that moves today. It consisted of a generator, rechargeable battery, and an electric starter motor with electric lights thrown in as a bonus. The radio came later. Gone were the hand cranks, magnetos, dry cell primary batteries, and flame headlamps. Fitted as standard equipment on the 1910 Cadillac, it was an immediate success, especially with women, and sales grew dramatically over the next few years, frequently doubling annually. It also allowed Cadillac to develop a more powerful, smoother six cylinder engine and its reputation as a luxury leader. By 1914, virtually every car offered an electric starter and the Kettering electric system. This very same year he began work on another new product, which we will come back to in a moment.

In 1916, Kettering sold Delco to United Motors Service, which was bought two years later by General Motors, and he established a new company, Dayton Research Laboratories. In 1920, General Motors bought his new company and in 1925 moved it to Detroit where it became the General Motors Research Laboratories. Kettering became the vice president of research. His unbounded curiosity, immense intellect, and perhaps most importantly his humanity allowed him to inspire others to join in a series of technical achievements which have become commonplace and accepted in a broad range of disciplines, including literally thousands of major advancements that we take for granted today. For his achievements, Kettering was awarded 21 honorary doctorates of science, belonged to 35 scientific societies covering a range of disciplines, and participated in most of them in leadership roles. Along with his duties at General Motors, he was either director or executive at 12 major corporations or institutions. In cooperation with Alfred P. Sloan, he established the Sloan-Kettering Institute, which has become the nation's leading cancer research facility.

In April of 1916, the first issue of "Delco-Light Flashes" announces effort to make electricity available to every farm.

But back to 1914, when his work on the automotive electric system of the future was nearly complete and being mass produced, he turned his interest to providing power to a rural America hungry for electricity. In the process, he created an entire industry of competitors and allied products. Hundreds of thousands of professional, office, manufacturing, sales, and service jobs across the nation were created over the next 40 years before sadly being lost to obscurity. It's astounding how so few people today know much about Kettering's contribution of bringing electricity to rural America and beyond. His electric plant had a dramatic impact on the lives on American farms and those who lived or worked in remote places, including Canada, Mexico, Australia, and 57 other countries that would ultimately benefit from his invention. That this enterprise, which contributed so much to the success of one of America's largest corporations and to many associated industries, has been lost to history is truly unfortunate. Kettering wanted to improve rural life and bring the joy and safety of electric lights and the convenience of running water and household appliances to his mother's rural home and other farm families. Thus he developed the Delco-Light Farm Electric Plant.

"All the advantages of an automatic Delco-Light combined with all the advantages of a storage battery."

The Delco-Light plant is a hybrid electric power plant. It is similar in function to the power train in modern hybrid vehicles that have become increasingly popular for their high efficiency. A small engine coupled to a generator (an engine-generator set, or "genset," as we will refer to it) is combined with a rechargeable battery to provide a continuous supply of electricity. In joining the genset to the battery as a system, the advantage of either power source is optimized and the disadvantages of each are minimized. When it's called on to operate, the genset runs at its most efficient point in terms of fuel efficiency, reliability, and life, whether it is supplying power directly or charging the batteries. The battery accepts and stores energy and supplies power silently for the times between when the genset is called on to start and run. The battery also is capable of supplying very high electric demand that could be several times the maximum capability of the genset. The engine automatically starts when the battery becomes discharged or if a lot of power is being drawn during periods of high electric use. When the batteries are full or the large demand is reduced, the engine shuts down automatically to wait for the next call for power.

One of three truly amazing aspects of this endeavor is that Kettering not only developed an electric power plant but an entire family of them capable of supplying a variety of needs from a summer cabin and farm to a country club and small town. By 1917, Delco-Light plants were available in 25 models with gensets from 500 to 3,000 watts, with a selection of properly sized batteries for each model. The variety of sizes made them popular not only on farms but for remote resorts, rural schools, churches, country clubs, outposts, camps, estates, and even yachts. However, over time the most popular unit became the 850-watt, 32-volt model that was optimized for the family farm. It would account for nearly 75 percent of production. The larger Delco-Light models were also available using a 112 volt battery for country clubs, large resorts, and other higher power uses. These represented a small percentage of production.

Delco-Light engines were 4-cycle, air-cooled, valve-in-head designs, and the generator, which also served as a starter motor, was direct connected. The early models ran on gasoline, but later ones used kerosene which was safer to store. The large flywheel drew air across the generator and engine for efficient

Twenty five models, easy payments, $250 complete for cabins, $295 for the small farm, less 6 percent cash.

cooling. It was fitted with a positive crankcase ventilation system, 50 years before cars began to use them, which returned crankcase gases to the engine for more complete combustion before being exhausted to the outdoors. This feature allowed the engine to run indoors in the basement. I am not so sure this would be acceptable today, but it seemed to work fine at the time. The large and very rugged engine operated smoothly and fairly quietly at a relatively slow speed of about 1,200 rpm. Delco-Light claimed an expected engine life of over 42 years in normal operations based on extensive simulated testing.

The battery consisted of 16 lead-acid, deep-cycle type cells in large glass containers. They were made especially for Delco by Exide, which would become a leading name in storage batteries in the 20th century. The lead-acid stationary battery is a remarkable device. It silently and efficiently accepts and supplies electric power year after year for as many as 15 to 20 years at which time it can be fully recycled and returned to service again and again. In fact, the lead-acid battery is today the most highly recycled product – over 98 percent. The next closest is the aluminum can which is a little over 60 percent. If kept in a warm place, say 60 to 80 degrees Fahrenheit, out of site and free from vibration, it could provide years of reliable service with little or no attention required.

Safe electric lamps, running water, and work-saving appliances for the modern farm from a dependable Delco-Light electric plant - a product of General Motors

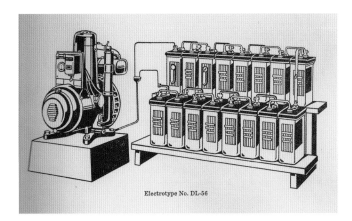

Electrotype No. DL-56

Delco designed and manufactured an engine and direct coupled generator with a storage battery to supply electricity.

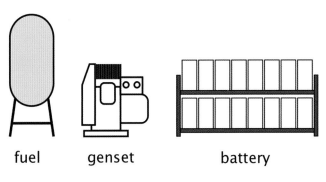

fuel   genset   battery

The basic farm electric plant converted kerosene in the genset to electricity for direct use or storage in the battery.

The large Delco-Light operated quietly at a slow speed with controls and a fuel tank mounted on the genset. *Courtesy of Wayne "Dr. Delco" Sphar, Avella, Pennsylvania.*

Delco-Light chose the quality Exide Ironclad battery for "best results."

A High Grade Set of Fixtures at a Remarkable Price

These Fixtures Are Shipped With Glassware, Wired and Assembled Complete, Ready to Install

A choice of six lighting fixtures, anywhere you wanted them, were included in the completely installed price.

An item to note is that Kettering designed his entire system to operate at 32 volts using direct current. He contended that it was absolutely safe, and he was correct. During the engineering phase from 1913 to 1915, 32 volts was chosen purely for safety against shock hazards. Early product literature proudly states: "Delco-Light 32 volt service is safe. There is no danger of serious or fatal shocks. Tests have shown that it requires 40 volts to break through the skin tissue." Kettering was way ahead of his time, very conscious of the well being of people and very attuned with the state of scientific understanding of this issue. History would prove him right on this point.

A second amazing aspect of Kettering's plan was the simultaneous introduction of a complete line of electric equipment and appliances to operate with the Delco-Light plant. In and of itself, the Delco-Light plant displayed a bit of genius, but Kettering knew he needed more items to go along with it, other than just light bulbs. First, he knew it was essential for these electric plants to be able to provide running water in order to be successful. The problem was there were no electric well pump manufacturers, so he designed both a shallow and a deep well pump system for use with his electric plants. His deep well pump was able to be used at depths of nearly 300 feet. Still Kettering knew a water pump was not enough either.

With DELCO PUMPS and WATER SYSTEMS
← for Convenience and Comfort →

COMFORT

PROFITABLE

CLEANLINESS

Delco Pumps and Water Systems supply water under pressure at the turn of a tap . . . They operate entirely automatically and will pump water from well, lake, cistern, stream or spring from a depth as low as 375 feet. The capacity of these Delco pumps more than meets normal water requirements as they deliver from 250 to 600 gallons of water per hour.

Delco Pumps are economical in operation, as well as initial cost. They will pump more than 100 gallons of water for less than one cent. They are durable, dependable and efficient.

Designed and manufactured by the pioneers of rural electrification, with over 15 years experience in pump manufacturing . . . Warranted against defective material and workmanship with a written guarantee . . . Made with selected materials

by experienced workmen with modern tools and machinery . . . Tested and inspected with precision tools and gauges.

The skill of experienced designers and workmen is reflected in the construction of Delco Pumps . . . The shallow well models are double-acting, pumping water on both forward and return strokes . . . self-priming, because suction opening is

above level of valves which are slotted . . . non-corrosive valve seats, made of brass . . . specially treated piston leathers, impervious to water . . . seamless pump cylinder of heavy brass tubing . . . self aligning, V-type endless belt . . . oversize, 3 piece packing box.

Separate water end permits accessibility of valves and inexpensive repairs . . . Eccentric drive minimizes wear because of large, ground bearing surface . . . splash lubrication . . . automatic switch, non-arcing contacts with safety device . . . brass relief valve . . . silent repulsion-induction type motor . . . hot dipped galvanized tank . . . air volume control.

Slow speed insures minimum wear and long life . . . compactness of design, positive drive and correct lubrication insures efficiency.

CONVENIENCE

SANITARY

LABOR SAVING

Running water - comfortable, convenient, clean, sanitary, labor-saving, profitable

A MODEL TO MEET YOUR REQUIREMENTS · ·

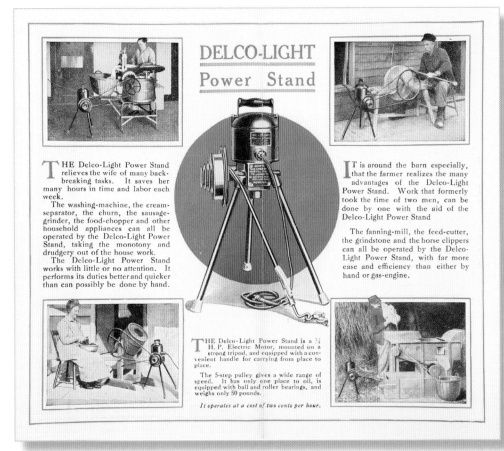

The portable Delco power stand allowed the farmer to operate all his powered equipment from a single device.

Many farms required mechanical power for a variety of uses, so he developed the quarter horsepower Delco-Light power stand, which included an electric motor and a set of gear-driven pulley sheaves on a portable tripod. The power stand provided belt-driven power to a variety of farm devices, such as milking machines, butter churns, fanning mills, feed cutters, grindstones, and other popular devices of the time.

The power stand made the farmer happy, but Kettering wanted the farm home to be fitted with all the modern electric conveniences that were becoming popular and an important part of life. Toward this end, he made the Delco-Light electric washer for clothes. Soon a complete line of popular home appliances made by Delco and others was available, including vacuum cleaners - both upright and hand, coffee makers, mixers, toasters, chafing dishes, curlers, heating pads, baby bottle warmers, waffle irons, clothes irons, radios, refrigerators, and motors. Everything operated on 32-volt direct current electricity.

Delco-Light washer forces soap and water through the clothes for a cleaner clean.

Exceptionally light and perfectly balanced, the Delco vacuum cleaner put an end to pushing dirt around.

THE DELCO HAND CLEANER

THE DELCO HAND CLEANER is invaluable for cleaning automobile interiors, over-stuffed furniture, curtains, drapes and stairs, as well as mattresses.

The slender nozzle with its soft rubber guard, is especially designed to reach into cramped, awkward corners and out-of-the-way places.

Finger-tip control . . . custom built, polished maple handle . . . compact, light in weight and well balanced . . . large opening dust bag easily removed . . . twenty-three feet of rubber covered non-kinkable cord—all of which allows you to do a quicker, better cleaning job, without the usual effort and fatigue.

As time went by Kettering's breakthough work with freon refrigerants led to the creation of a Delco-Light subsidiary to build refrigerators. Frigidaire propelled General Motors into a leadership position in the electric appliance business for the next few decades. Frigidaire made refrigerators for cities in the U.S. and exported a large number of them to other countries. And of course, they offered a 32-volt direct current model for use with Delco-Light plants.

By the spring of 1916, Kettering had designed a family of electric power plants with a complete selection of the most popular electrical appliances and devices. The final amazing aspect was that he built a huge factory employing thousands of people to make this equipment, established a strong partnership with a great battery company, and created an incredible marketing, sales, distribution, dealer, installation, and service organization all before he sold his first Delco-Light plant. Sales of the Delco-Light plant took off immediately and expanded significantly. By the fifth year, more than 175,000 units were in service throughout the United States, Canada, and Mexico.

The Delco-Light plant was a remarkable accomplishment on its own, but the huge demand it created fostered stiff competition. In 1921, there were 72 other companies offering 32-volt farm electric plants and dozens more selling related equipment. By 1935, the number grew to 156. Companies that built engines added generators, while at the same time companies that made generators added engines. A few of the most successful continued to grow and expand to become familiar names we know today.

The Delco hand vacuum was perfect for those small clean-up jobs and spills.

Here are the features *that insure* Radio Reception equal to AMERICA'S FINEST RADIO SETS

COMPARE these desirable features of the new United Motors 32-volt Home Radio—point by point—and you will discover for yourself that this is the radio of greatest value. In fact, the chassis—and the genuine super-heterodyne circuit—are designed and built by the foremost radio engineers in the country; and they incorporate many new developments not found in any other receiving set.

1. Perfected short wave feature, bringing in police, amateur, government, and aviation broadcasts. A small switch, on the face of the set, opens up the low wave bands.

2. Operates from standard 32-volt storage battery without requiring dry cell or any other battery.

3. Tubeless full wave eliminator makes bothersome B batteries unnecessary.

4. Gives real all-electric performance; yet is economical due to low current consumption.

5. Automatic Volume Control prevents "fading," and "blasting" from nearby stations.

6. Tone Selector allows listener to choose the desired tone—through the full range from treble to bass.

7. Full electro-dynamic speaker, the finest type known, with improved cone type construction for added quality and range of tone.

8. Perfected sensitivity and selectivity. Permits ample reception distance without cross talk between stations.

9. Quiet tuning—no hum.

10. Superheterodyne circuit—most expensive to manufacture, but giving much superior performance.

11. New type tubes—giving the performance formerly obtainable only from 8 to 9 tube sets.

12. Non-glare, indirect illuminated tuning dial—graduated in kilocycles for quick location of stations.

13. The United Motors Home Radio is also ideally suited for installation in boats using 32-volt plants.

• • •

With the new United Motors 32-volt Home Radio, the broadcast *and* low wave bands are within your reach. You will find it most interesting to explore the short wave bands—as well as most pleasant to listen to the standard programs as this new radio brings them in.

The Table Model is popular wherever space is limited

Model 4049 is a beautifully designed, smartly modern model suitable for either the mantelpiece or a convenient table. Like the larger console, it is a masterpiece of cabinet workmanship that is worthy of the finest surroundings. It occupies no more table surface than the ordinary reading lamp; yet it brings into your home every radio program you care to hear—and brings them with the volume and quality of the most expensive sets.

The front panel is attractively overlaid with straight grained, matched walnut veneer. The modern, graceful pilasters are neatly decorated with black-vein lines and a beautiful inlay.

Table Model 4049 . . . $64.50

The New UNITED MOTORS *home* RADIO
FOR 32 VOLT CURRENT

The United Motors radio was a must have for the modern farm.

A full range of 32-volt direct current convenience appliances were available in stores or mail order catalogs.

The efficient Frigidaire refrigerator made by Delco was available for 32-volt direct current operation as well as for city electricity.

The Delco-Light factory in Dayton, Ohio, would grow to 1.3 million square feet of floor space.
From the collection of Dayton History, Dayton, Ohio.

A first class dealer network would insure a professional installation for dependable service - rail freight paid east of the Mississippi.

Fairbanks-Morse, founded in 1823, initially started with Eclipse windmills for water pumping and became known for scales used to weigh freight and large items. The company evolved into a diversified manufacturer by the early 1900s, and began making engines. Fairbanks-Morse began production of its model Z engine in 1914, and built an estimated 500,000 of these popular engines. A very large number of these engines were coupled with a generator on a frame and sold as the Fairbanks-Morse Farm Light Plant.

Kohler Co., a leading manufacturer of plumbing fixtures, made a line of farm electric plants beginning in the early 1920s and continues to make both small air-cooled engines and gensets from 6 kilowatts to 3,250 kilowatts for a variety of applications, including prime and emergency power, marine, RV, mobile, fire and rescue, and home standby. Tens of thousands of Kohler generator sets were put into service on farms and for cabins, resorts, and commercial buildings during the company's early history.

Similarly, David Onan started making the "10 light generator" in 1925 and began manufacturing small engines in 1930. The Onan model 123L-5 genset, rated at 1,260 watts/32 volts direct current, was private labeled to many firms, such as Fairbanks-Morse and Winpower, for farm light plants. This small, lightweight, and dependable genset became extremely popular during its nearly 30 years in production. Today the Onan Corp., which is owned by the Cummins Engine Co., remains a leading manufacturer of generator sets worldwide.

The entire Delco-Light sales and marketing operation was run out of the General Motors headquarters building in Detroit under the United Motors Service name. For the next 20 years, Delco-Light plant sales grew, even during the Great Depression, and production approached 400,000 units. By 1930, nearly 10 percent of rural America was electrified and the number was growing as new competitors became involved. Several thousand people worked for Delco-Light in Dayton, Ohio, and later in Rochester, New

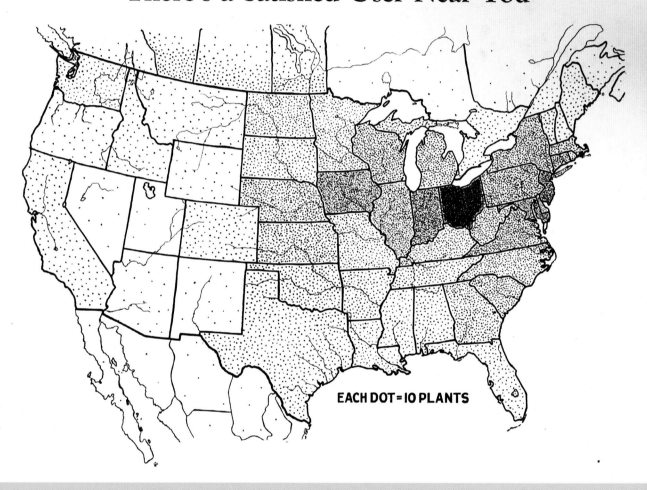

Dependable DELCO·LIGHT

"There's a Satisfied User Near You"

EACH DOT = 10 PLANTS

The sales map tells it all, 175,000 units in five years. Each dot represents ten Delco-Light plants installed. *Courtesy of the Scharchburg Archives, Kettering University, Flint, Michigan.*

York. With the jobs created among its competitors, battery and appliance manufacturers, retailers, and installation/service providers, the business could have easily counted for hundreds of thousands of jobs. New competition was about to come along in the form of wind-driven generators and the federal government would follow with an ill-conceived program – the Rural Electrification Act of 1936 – that would destroy the entire industry.

The effects in the industry were felt immediately and farm electric plant sales slowed. The call to support the war effort would be answered by most of these companies in the early 1940s. By the end of World War II most of the companies changed product lines and ultimately closed their farm electric plant operations. Delco-Light production ended in 1947.

"**And the Earth replied tis Delco-Light.**" *From the collection of Dayton History, Dayton, Ohio.*

A great era and legacy comes to an end, soon forgotten and lost to time.

Chapter 5

WIND ELECTRIC PLANTS

The radio was a must to have for everyone when introduced in the 1920s.

In the early 1920s, the electrical technology paths of brain and brawn, telecommunications and power, came together again. The telegraph gave way to the telephone, and now the new "wireless" had arrived in the form of the radio. In a strange twist of fate, we find Thomas Edison's General Electric Corp. acquiring patent rights from Guglielmo Marconi that had been taken from Nikola Tesla, and forming the Radio Corporation of America (RCA). Competing against him was his old rival George Westinghouse and the Westinghouse Broadcasting Corp. and a newcomer out of Alexander Bell's American Telegraph and Telephone Co. (AT&T). They eventually joined together to form the National Broadcasting Co. (NBC). At any rate, broadcasts began in earnest, and Americans could not have been more captivated and compelled to have their own radios. The major issue was lack of electric power in most rural and remote parts of the country. These were the people who did not have a Delco-Light or other farm electric plant yet.

Radio enthusiasts on farms and in remote places used car batteries for power. When those batteries lost their charge, they took them to the service station in town to be recharged. This often arduous and inconvenient task got old quickly. In the most remote farm areas in the Great Plains where farming was a real struggle, people had to rely more on their ingenuity to get their power. A few inventors came up with a creative solution. They took a 6 or 12 volt automobile generator, carved an airplane propeller out of wood, bolted it to the front of the generator, attached a long rod with a tail to point the blade into the wind, and set it on a post. This was the birth of the homemade wind generator. Now radio batteries could be charged by the constant wind. In addition, the wind generator might produce enough power to add a few light bulbs and further increase the joy of evening radio.

During the next 10 to 15 years, more than 20 wind generator manufacturers brought more sophisticated and larger units to the market and expanded their businesses through the Depression years. From the early radio chargers, wind generators quickly grew in size, not only to compete with the Delco-Light and other farm electric plants, but to operate in conjunction with them to reduce fuel use. Some wind generators were so successful that many farmers found they met all of their electric needs, and fuel use was completely eliminated.

Beyond the cities, an automobile generator, wood propeller, and tail became a wind generator to charge a radio battery and run a few light bulbs.

Larger wind generators to supply an entire household were developed to compete with farm electric plants or save fuel for homes with them.

Of all the wind generator manufacturers of the era, a few stood out for their technical and business accomplishments and are worthy of a more detailed understanding.

The Jacobs Wind Electric Co. was perhaps the most significant and remarkable. The year was 1924 at a place called Vida, Montana, a desolate location near the North Dakota border. Here, brothers Charlie, Joe, Marcellus, and Fred Jacobs were caught up in the national fascination with radio and were building their own receivers. Using their mother's clothesline as an antenna, they listened to broadcasts from as far away as Los Angeles. They sold these receivers to their neighbors to earn money to build a shortwave broadcast station and became known as the "Voice of Cow Creek." Powered by a 32-volt farm electric plant, the Jacobs brothers broadcasted evenings and on the weekends, telling jokes, making up skits, and having their friends play musical instruments for the benefit of the neighbors. They eventually sold the transmitter to a friend, but not before Joe invented an electronic pick-up arm for the new hand crank phonograph, a technological breakthrough that became the industry standard. Marcellus and Joe soon after turned their interest to wind-driven generators for charging radio batteries and developed a small unit for sale. But the brothers had bigger ideas and set out to develop a large wind generator to compete

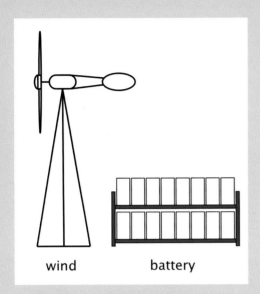

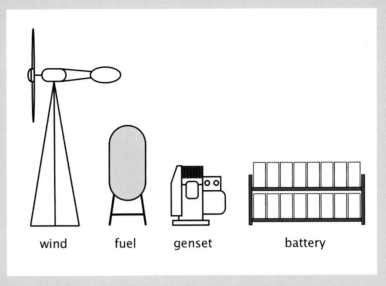

A wind electric plant combined a wind driven generator and battery to supply electricity.

Wind generators were frequently used with farm electric plants to reduce fuel and have an assured supply of electricity year round.

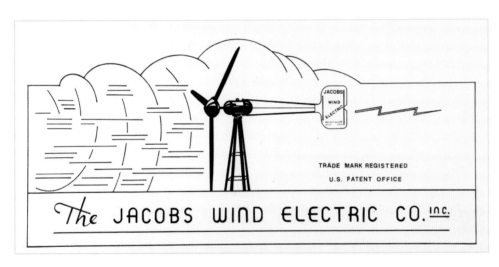

The Jacobs Wind Electric Co. quickly became the premier manufacturer of a legendary wind generator and leading supplier of wind electric plants.

with the 32-volt home electric plants developed by Delco-Light and others.

After experimenting for a few years, Marcellus, who would become known in the industry as M. L., and Joe settled on a final design and started to manufacture it. They moved to Minneapolis in 1930 to open a factory. In 1931, the first Jacobs Model 45 units began to roll off the production line. The Model 45's design was a success, and the brothers soon added the Model 60, which was identical to its predecessor except for a slightly longer generator and an increased rating of 2,500 watts for more power where the winds were strong. All other parts of the Model 60 were identical and interchangeable with the Model 45.

Not only did they make all of the right basic decisions about the design of their windmill, they were committed to a concept that placed them ahead of any competitors. Their wind machine ran smoothly, reliably, and efficiently day after day, year after year, decade after decade unattended in all weather conditions. Jacobs Wind Electric Plants quickly became legendary for their flawless performance and total reliability, with virtually no breakdowns or maintenance required. This incredible feat was the hallmark of their success and is to this day a fundamental concept that must be adhered to for successful wind generators. I have personally removed several of them from towers after decades of operation, performed simple rebuilds, and put them back in service without ever experiencing a single problem. Let's take a closer look at this magnificent machine.

Marcellus L. Jacobs with the dependable Jacobs Model 60 wind generator.

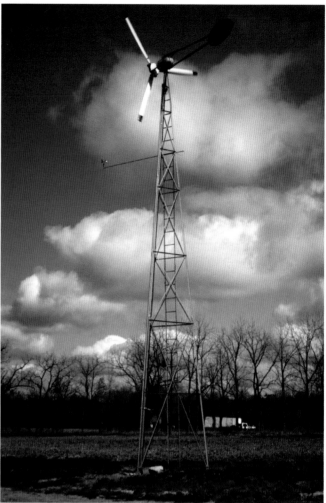

Restored Jacobs Model 45 on a 35-foot Wincharger tower

The Model 45 was one of the larger wind generators produced in its time. It had a three-blade propeller with a 15-foot diameter. It was direct-connected to a large slow-speed generator rated at 45 amps and 40 volts for a maximum output of 1,800 watts. (Note: Although the farm electric plants were rated 32 volts nominal, their actual voltage would vary with the battery state of charge and charge/discharge rate between 27 and 38 volts. The generator had to produce more than the higher voltage of 38 and thus the 40-volt generator rating. For the rest of the book, we will simply refer to the nominal battery voltage.)

The three blades, made of aircraft quality Sitka spruce, were attached to a flyball actuated governor which limited the speed of the propellers to a maximum of 225 rpm no matter how strong the winds blew. It did this by changing the angle or pitch of the blades equally to convert the "lift" forces that propelled or accelerated them to "drag" forces which slowed them down. If you could stand at the base of a tower in complete calm and slowly increase the wind speed you would see the Model 45 start to turn slowly when the speed reached about 10 mph. It should be noted that, once running, the Model 45 would continue to operate in winds as low as 7 mph. As wind speeds increase, the propeller speed increases from 125 rpm until it turns at 225 rpm in a 22 mph wind. At this point, the weight of the fly-balls overcome a spring preload and turn the blades simultaneously into a stall condition, the propeller slows down and the fly-balls retract, and the process continues repeatedly no matter how high the wind speed goes until it slows down again below 22 mph. I watched this process one stormy evening on one of my Model 45 units in winds measured at 98 mph. In the harshest conditions around the world, the same stories emerged. Put up a Model 45 and it works unattended for decades and never fails.

A huge contribution to the success of the Model 45 that came from Jacobs' early experiments was their conclusion that three blades is the right number for a high efficiency wind-driven generator. M. L. would speak on this subject to anybody who

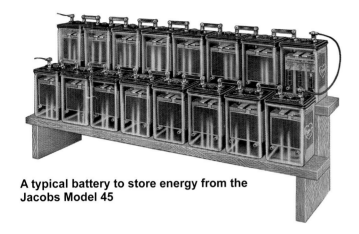

A typical battery to store energy from the Jacobs Model 45

Jacobs Model 45 spinning smoothly, quietly, efficiently in a moderate wind

A Jacobs Wind Electric Plant became a common site on farms, especially those that were the last to receive the "high line."

brought it up - he was not shy. He was right for many reasons. The three-blade system simply operates more smoothly since it's always in perfect mass and aerodynamic balance regardless of the position of the blades. Secondly, because of this, the turning rotor can easily be oriented to face the wind with a smooth transition as it adjusts to the inevitably constantly changing wind direction. Finally, they start up faster from a rest position after a period of calm. In the stopped position, one blade is straight up and the other two are at 30 degrees below horizontal so that all of them are in "clean" air. With a two-blade machine, the static position would be straight up and down with the lower blade directly in front of the tower in disturbed air. With a four-blade machine the lower blade would have the same conditions and three of the four would provide a disproportionate part of the start-up torque required.

One other feature that is worth mentioning is that the propeller blades were upwind of the tower and were pointed into the wind by a tail-vane mounted behind the generator. As a matter of convenience, the position of the tail-vane could be controlled from the ground to turn the wind generator off by placing the rotor sideways to the wind. Although most wind generators incorporate this feature, the Jacobs had a slightly different approach that demonstrated their wisdom. With the Model 45, the tail-vane's normal position is "off" and you had to turn the tail-vane to the "on" position behind the generator to point the rotor into the wind. This was accomplished by connecting the tail-vane by a chain, wire, and swivel down through the turntable to a crank handle mounted on one of the tower legs near the ground. The other wind generators had a similar mechanism except the normal position would be "on" and it had to be turned "off" at the ground. If the cable failed, the Jacobs

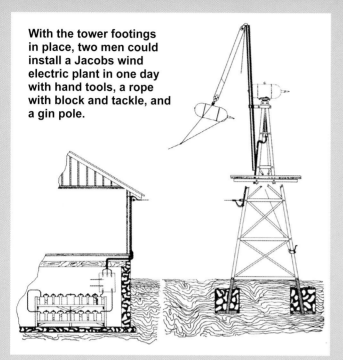

With the tower footings in place, two men could install a Jacobs wind electric plant in one day with hand tools, a rope with block and tackle, and a gin pole.

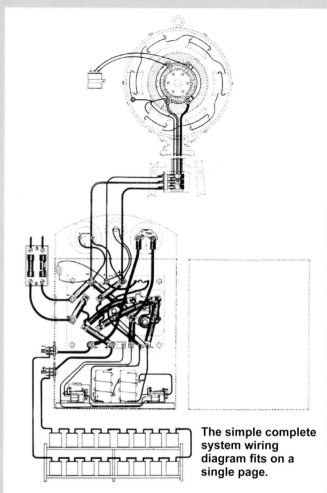

The simple complete system wiring diagram fits on a single page.

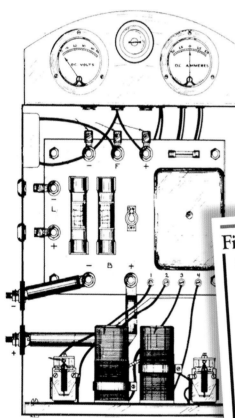

The Jacobs "Master-mind" automatic control panel regulated power from the wind generator to the batteries and the home.

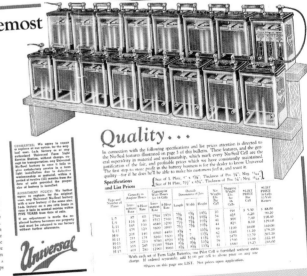

Typically, the battery would be mounted on a wood rack and placed in the basement of the home.

Model 45 would turn itself off, whereas if the cable failed on other machines, they would be impossible to turn off, especially during a storm.

When production began in 1932, a Jacobs Model 45 included the wind generator, a large 32-volt battery, a "Master-Mind" control system, and a 50-foot tower for a cost of $595. The Master-Mind control system regulated power from the generator to optimize charging of the battery. Unlike the competition, which normally used a simple cut out relay, the Jacobs Master-Mind sensed when the battery was close to full-charged and would reduce charge rate to a slow "trickle" to "equalize" the cells, improving performance and extending battery life. In the Master-Mind panel, a manual override switch served two purposes. Instructions specified that when the wind electric plant was first installed, the override switch should be turned on and the wind generator be allowed to give the battery a strong overcharge with no power drawn off. The wind generator should then be turned off and the battery fully discharged before turning the wind generator back on and returning the override switch to the off position for normal operation. It was also recommended that the override switch be turned on every two months in strong winds to provide an overcharge to break up sulphation in the battery to restore and maintain capacity and extend life. With this procedure Jacobs was able to provide an unconditional 10-year warranty on their battery, as opposed to the three year which was the industry standard at the time. The batteries would typically last 12 to 20 years and would be recycled, of course.

The battery was a string of 16 large lead-acid cells in glass containers and specially designed for deep cycle farm electric plant service. M.L. Jacobs had cells made to his specification by Willard Battery in Cleveland, a large supplier to the auto industry at the time, with the Jacobs name on them and sold them with an unconditional 10-year warranty. The standard size rating was 440 ampere-hours with an optional 660 ampere-hours battery available for heavy use with a Model 60 in strong wind areas. These two sizes would store 14 kilowatt hours and 21 kilowatt hours, respectively, which would continue to supply electric power for a period of two or three days to perhaps as long as a week in calm wind, which was rare in the Great Plains. In practice, there were several battery manufacturers competing for the farm electric plant business, and the Jacobs wind generator could be used with batteries from any of the manufacturers.

The standard Jacobs tower was a 50-foot four-post type that was popular with the ubiquitous farm multi-blade water pumping windmill. In fact, Jacobs bought their towers from windmill manufacturers in the Midwest, such as Challenge, Dempster, and Woodmanse. Jacobs even allowed their wind plants to be used with a three-post tower made by an arch competitor. The standard 50-foot tower was more than adequate for most farms on the Great Plains, where they were the most popular and the highest surface obstructions were wheat fields and fence posts. Other tower heights ranging from 30 feet to 80 feet were available for areas from completely flat and barren to tree covered.

Always looking for new and innovative products and opportunities, the Jacobs brothers teamed up with Briggs and Stratton to make their own 2.5 kilowatt gasoline genset to be sold with their wind electric plants. They would go on to offer a larger 6 kilowatt diesel genset, too. These machines would insure a continuous supply of electric power even for large uses during extremely long periods of calm wind. Like everything they did, these gensets were top-notch.Jacobs even offered high efficiency freezers and refrigerators for use with their plants. In fact, their freezers had cork insulation, and M. L. would often brag "that you could turn the power off and ice cream would stay hard for a week," as he gave them away on television shows, like Queen for a Day, in the 1950s.

The Jacobs wind plant was an instant success and sales grew rapidly. Combined with propane for home heat, hot water, and cooking, all the modern home conveniences were now available for rural and remote families. Jacobs advertising literature promised energy production of 300 to 500 kilowatt hours per month in strong winds. That's a lot of energy. When I collected the Jacobs plants from remote farms in the 1970s, the farmers were very gracious. They were happy to talk with me and would invite me in for dinner. They were curious about the future of their wind generators, and I was likewise curious about their experiences. One of these farm families had a Jacobs Wind Electric Plant and all of the possible modern appliances. In addition, the farmer had several motorized pieces of equipment that he frequently used. I asked the family if the wind generator produced enough power for their needs. They replied that it produced too much power and the battery was always fully charged. So they adapted by turning the wind generator on one or two days each week to charge the battery. Once the battery was charged, they turned the Jacobs' tail-vane to the off position for a few days until the "lights dimmed a little" and the wind plant was then reactivated. They never ran their genset. It was a very windy area.

A Jacobs Wind Electric Plant was the primary source of electricity for Admiral Byrd's Little America camp at the South Pole.

A special Jacobs wind generator was developed to prevent oil and gas pipelines from corroding and was used around the world.

Admiral Richard Byrd's Little America expedition took a Jacobs Wind Electric Plant with a 70-foot tower, an Exide iron-clad battery, and a Kohler light plant for power. Byrd and his engineers wrote M. L. and spoke glowingly about how flawlessly the wind generator operated through the entire expedition, also noting that the wind generator supplied all the power most of the time saving them precious genset fuel. Wind speeds in the area measured in excess of 100 miles per hour and temperatures dipped to 100 degrees Fahrenheit below zero, and there was not a single failure from the Jacobs during the entire expedition. When the expedition returned in 1947 and again in 1955, the wind plant was still fully operable.

The weather station at Eureka on Ellesmere Island inside the Arctic Circle was also powered by a Jacobs wind plant. A mission in Ethiopia installed a Jacobs in 1938 and they wrote M. L. in 1968 to inform him that they only needed a small $5 wear item, armature brushes, to keep their plant running.

M. L. developed a special low voltage model especially to provide cathodic protection to underground pipelines. His clients included most of the major gas and oil companies in the United States and Saudi Arabia. Add a special unit for the railroads

and remote runways and Jacobs Wind Electric Plants were showing up in countries throughout the world, such as Spain, South Africa, many South American countries, and islands just about everywhere.

During the 1940s, Jacobs bought out many competitors and, like others, contributed the company's skills to the war effort. Jacobs made a "degaussing" unit for ship hulls that was based on the 6-kilowatt diesel set to help protect against magnetic mines at sea. A 110-volt version of the Model 60 wind generator, the so-called Model 60BX, was introduced with a 3,000 watt rating. A new and improved governor system to replace the venerable flyball governor was developed and became a standard by 1950. Jacobs would outlast most of its competitors and in the later years would acquire a few of them, such as Universal Battery Co. and Nelson Electric Co., which the company renamed Allied Electric Co. Jacobs had a great reputation and a continuing demand for their wind generators through the mid-1950s. In 1960, the factory closed and the land was ultimately used for the construction of Interstate 94, north of downtown Minneapolis. M. L. Jacobs, the surviving brother, moved to Fort Myers, Florida to plan his comeback in the 1970s and 1980s, while he developed a residential waterfront subdivision named Island Park.

Wincharger Corp. became a fierce competitor to Jacobs and started from simple beginnings at about the same time the Jacobs brothers began their interest in wind generators. Another pair of brothers worked along similar lines about 700 miles southeast in Cherokee, Iowa. In 1927, John and Gerhard Albers started Albers Propeller Co. and developed a small wind generator called the "Wincharger" to charge 6 and 12 volt radio batteries. The Wincharger was a local hit. The company grew to three employees and produced six Winchargers a day. One day in 1935, executives from the Zenith Radio Corp. placed an order for 50,000 Winchargers and took a 51 percent stake in the new Wincharger Corp. The small Wincharger unit would become the most produced wind generator over the next 60 plus years, and Wincharger would immediately become an important force in the new wind electric plant market. Within a year, the Wincharger moved to a larger 30,000-square-foot plant in nearby Sioux City, had 52 full time employees, and was producing 200 Winchargers a day. In time, production soared to 2,000 units a day at a price of

The railroads bought a lot of Jacobs Wind Electric Plants for their remote power needs.

Marcellus Jacobs, or M. L. to his friends, with a model of his famous wind generator in 1985

slip ring assembly and mounting feet for easy installation on the roof of an outbuilding were included. It was not a good idea to mount the Wincharger on the roof of the house, since it would act as a sounding board to the point of being intolerable. Wires connected the generator to a simple relay panel in the house and to the radio battery. When the wind blew, the battery would charge and the radio would provide continuous entertainment on demand. Since the battery was usually kept charged, the owner would frequently add a few light bulbs to make good use of the abundant wind energy.

Before too long, a larger 32-volt, direct-drive model with an 8-foot diameter propeller rated at 650 watts was offered to the farm electric plant market. This model was similar in all respects to the small model and sold for $69.95, plus tower and battery, when it was first introduced. But bigger would not be big enough for the Albers brothers, and a new larger gear-driven generator with an 11-foot diameter propeller, a 1,200-watt rating, and a movable tail vane that could be used to turn it out of the wind went into production within a few years. The Wincharger "Giant"

$44 apiece, or even better at $10 per unit less with the additional purchase of a Zenith radio. Zenith bought the remaining 49 percent of WIncharger and continued to sell the wind generators to farms with their radios.

The original Wincharger unit had a two-blade, upwind, direct-drive design. A single 6-foot-long Douglas fir, 1-inch-by-4-inch board was shaped to the company's patented air foil propeller specifications and fitted with their patented air brake governor. These components were attached by a drum brake plate to the generator. At wind speeds above 20 mph, the flaps which would normally travel in a circle would extend out to counteract the propeller forces and limit the speed up to a point. Prudent Wincharger owners would apply the brake when severe weather approached. A tail vane was fixed in place by a length of angle iron to the back of the generator to point it into the wind. A small four-post tower with a turntable and

The Wincharger Corp. started with a radio wind generator and added larger models for full farm electric service.
Courtesy of George Greenhough/www.wincharger.com.

You are invited To a Special Showing of NEW ECONOMICAL

ZENITH

FARM RADIOS Operated by Frepower from the air!

DeLUXE
WINCHARGER

—And the Genuine
6-Volt DeLuxe

WINCHARGER
REG. U.S. PAT. OFF.

STOP Spending Money for
DRY BATTERIES!

•

END ALL Recharging
Nuisance!

•

ONLY 50c A YEAR
Power Operating Cost!

Complete with 6-foot propeller, air-cooled generator-auto-type brake, strong 5½-foot steel tower, and instrument panel.

SPECIAL PRICE
Only

$15 00

with new
6-Volt
Zenith
Farm Radio

The 1,200 watt gear-driven Wincharger "Giant" with a 12-foot propeller increased energy production at an economical price.

would compete with the larger wind generators. The less expensive gear-driven design gave them an important price advantage over direct-drive systems, and they competed effectively in the burgeoning farm electric market. An upgraded enclosed control panel was included which had provisions for connecting a 32-volt Delco-Light or other genset. The Giant would evolve over time by replacing the air brake governor with two additional blades, giving the new model four blades made of aluminum. The pitch of the two additional blades was controlled by a flyball governor mechanism, but the control strategy was the same - two blades with "lift" counteracted by two blades with "drag."

Wincharger's batteries were manufactured to its specifications and with the company's name stamped on them. These batteries were available in six sizes from 126 ampere-hours (4 kilowatt hours) for the smaller models up to 424 ampere hours (13.5 kilowatt hours) for the Giant.

A 650 watt, 32 volt direct drive Wincharger was the first step up in size. *Courtesy of George Greenhough/www. wincharger.com.*

SELF-SUPPORTING

WINCHARGER

TOWER

EASIEST TO ERECT

No previous experience is needed to make a perfect job of erecting Wincharger Self-Supporting Tower. Every part fits together perfectly. Each tower is furnished complete with Anchor Posts, Galvanized Erection Bolts and Lock Washers. Corner Posts, Angle Girts and Flat Braces for each section are packed in one bundle. All bolts, nuts and lock washers are in one bag. This makes it easy to lay out each section before starting to erect the tower.

Features THAT MEAN SOMETHING TO YOU

Design—A 3-post design which utilizes the triangle as the most successful method of resisting distortion. Tower legs are of a special 60 degree U-SHAPED design (Patent Pending) developed for Wincharger to give extra rigidity and strength.

Strong—Built for permanence. When the Anchor Plates are buried in concrete and the tower is properly erected it will withstand the heaviest winds. The special 60 degree leg sections are stronger than any other angle of the same weight.

Durable—All steel used in the manufacture of Wincharger Self-Supporting Tower is Hot Dip Galvanized after the holes are punched. Rust Proof prime grades of Spelter only are used in the galvanizing.

Rigid—Heavy girts or cross angles are spaced every five feet. A new brace tightening method involving a Bent Plate drawn to the tower legs by two bolts makes it easy to tighten the braces properly—and keep them tight.

Ladders—Safe and Strong. Climbing is made easy with steps spaced only 15" apart.

Platform—A strongly constructed and easily assembled wood platform is included with each order for Wincharger Sectional Tower. This platform makes it easy to bolt the Wincharger unit onto the tower and service the machine whenever it needs oiling or minor adjustments.

Anchors—Two angles 11" long, bolted to the anchor posts near the bottom, provide an adequate foundation when well buried in concrete.

The Wincharger tower was slender, rigid, elegant, and could easily be put up by one person in a morning. Courtesy of George Greenhough/www.wincharger.com.

Wincharger offered two types of towers for use with its wind generators. For the smaller models, a guyed-type tower was offered in 20-foot sections, up to 80 feet. Towers with guy wires to hold them up were significantly less expensive than freestanding towers, but they were vulnerable to the loss of any one of the guy wires. The freestanding tower that they developed was an absolute marvel and should serve as a model for modern use as it would be easy to adapt the design to larger machines. Conventional wind towers were typical four-post models made out of standard angle-iron. The Wincharger tower was a three-post model, for extra rigidity, and the legs were made into a special U-shaped design with overlaps formed into one end of each leg section to accept the mating section for a very strong joint design. Another innovative feature was a simple and effective tensioning scheme. With level footings extending underground, surrounded at the bottom by concrete and prepared the day before, one person could easily install a tower with a couple of spanner wrenches in three to four hours, leaving the afternoon to install the wind generator. Easy to level, erect, and tension, the Wincharger tower was very rigid and quiet, and it had a smaller footprint than four-post towers.

Over time, Wincharger became the volume leader. It was the longest continuously produced wind generator, and the company carried on by transitioning to other electrical generation products under the Winco name. During World War II, Winco made rotary inverters for the military and in the post war years transitioned to portable, stationary, and mobile generators and the original small radio wind generator. Winco still produces generating equipment and recently merged with Winpower, another early wind plant manufacturer.

Started as the Miller Motor Co. in 1925 to build wind-driven farm light plants exclusively, the company was purchased by Ed McCardell and his father in 1932 and renamed Wind Power Light Co, which it was known as until it became the Winpower Corporation in 1974. McCardell ran the company until 1975 and was a remarkable person and gifted engineer. The company produced its unique wind generator design until the early 1960s and although it was not noted for volume production or size, it had a loyal following of satisfied customers and everybody had something nice to say about it. I bought a few and was overwhelmed at what a thoughtful, effective design this machine represented.

The Wind Power Light machine, rated at 1,200 watts, was different from all the other wind generators in that it was a downwind design. With this type of design, the rotor is placed downwind of the tower and is used to orient it into the wind and thus eliminate the need for a tail vane. McCardell wisely choose three blades, which were 12 feet in diameter, and they had a very simple flyball mechanism and link to change the pitch equally on all the propellers when the maximum rpm was reached.

The generator was placed in front of the tower to counterbalance the weight of the governor and blades and allow the machine to "track" the changing wind direction effectively. The generator and rotor were connected to the ends of a long shaft with two large central bearings on either side of the center of the tower. A drum brake was mounted between the two bearings to allow the machine to be turned off or "stopped" by a cable and crank at the base of the tower. A compact turntable and slip ring assembly served to mount the wind generator and was, in turn, mounted on a long shaft that would allow the wind machine to be fine "leveled" even if the tower was a

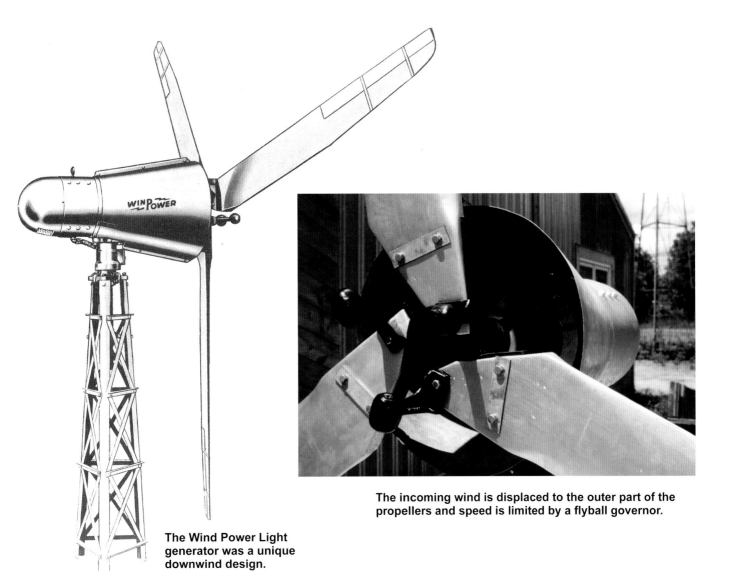

The Wind Power Light generator was a unique downwind design.

The incoming wind is displaced to the outer part of the propellers and speed is limited by a flyball governor.

little off. This was a very important factor. If a tower was not perfectly level, a wind generator would tend to lean with the tower when running and stop in the same off position when it was not turning.

One other aspect that I found particularly insightful was that the machine had a shroud between the generator and rotor that displaced the wind from the center of the rotor to the outer "working" area of the blades. If we looked at where the rotational forces are created with a rotor, we would find that all of these forces came from the outer two-thirds of each blade and that the inner third does not add any force and in fact is a drag on power. By moving the incoming wind from the center of the rotor, first by flowing over the generator and next the shroud, the speed of the wind would be increased and flow over the working part of each blade. The net effect was an overall increase in performance and efficiency.

Wind Power Light continued to produce a diversified selection of electric generating products from its 112,000 square-foot plant in Newton, Iowa, and would ultimately join up with its previous competitor Winco. Like every other manufacturer, Wind Power Light Company was a significant supplier of portable generators during and after World War II.

William Dunn, a prolific inventor began his career in manufacturing in 1917 when he founded Dunn Manufacturing Co. By 1934 his interest turned to wind generators and he found a ready market for his innovative radio charger design. In 1936, he joined up with C. L. Parris to form Parris-Dunn Corp. The innovative Parris-Dunn governing principle would tilt the rotor and generator up to reduce the rotor area from a circular disc to an ellipse, with a smaller area, as the wind speed increased and thus reduced the power. The rotor and generator also turned up 90 degrees to the off position by a cable that ran to a crank handle at the base of the tower. They called it the patented "slip the wind" governing principle. In addition to the two small 6 and 12 volt models rated

The innovative Parris-Dunn wind generator used the "slip the wind principle" with an offset pivot to allow it to tip up in strong winds to limit speed in strong winds. *Courtesy of George Greenhough/www.wincharger.com.*

"A size for every purse and purpose" – 6-, 12-, 32-, and 110-volt models with rated power of 135, 150, 400, 650, 1,000, 1,250, and 2,500 watts. *Courtesy of George Green-hough/www.wincharger.com.*

at 135 and 150 watts, there were three mid-size 12 and 32 volt models rated at 400 and 650 watts, and three larger 32 and 110 volt models with direct-drive designs and rated at 1,000 to 1,250 watts, all with two blades. Two extra large three-bladed models rated 2,500 to 3,000 watts were produced in the later years.

During World War II, Parris-Dunn had 250 employees and manufactured more than 2 million training rifles for the Army and Navy. The plant and business closed in 1949. In the short period between 1934 and 1941, over 37,000 Parris-Dunn wind plants were placed in service in the United States and 93 countries.

There are similar stories to be told about the other 18 manufacturers of wind generators in the 1930s and 1940s. However, due to their smaller size of operations and sales, their stories have been obscured and may never be fully told. A list of all the ones that I am aware of follows.

The overall effect of the farm electric plant era, encompassing the manufacturers of Delco-Light and all of the other gensets, wind generators, towers, battery sets, appliances, retailers, and installation and service people, was the employment of hundreds of thousands of people. It would be an oversight not to note that many of the jobs were technical and professional in nature and, due to the location of the manufacturing plants, allowed the children of farm families to remain in the area earning a good wage and contributing to their communities.

Universal Battery Co. acquired wind generator manufacturers before being bought itself by a wind generator manufacturer. *Courtesy of George Greenhough/ www.wincharger.com.*

During the 1930s and '40s, two dozen companies, primarily located in the midwest, were known to have manufactured and offered wind generators for sale in the farm electric plant market.

Wind Company	also known as	Town, State
Aer Zephyr		Spencer, Iowa
Aermotor		Chicago, Illinois
Aero-Electric		Spencer, Iowa
Air Electric Machine Co.	Wind Impeller Co.	Jewell, Iowa
Aerodyne	Aerolite	Minneapolis, Minnesota
C. H. Carlson		Minneapolis, Minnesota
Charles E. Miller Co.		Anderson, Indiana
Currier Manufacturing	Wesco	Minneapolis, Minnesota
Emil Magneson		Backoo, North Dakota
Fritschle		Denver, Colorado
Jacobs Wind Electric Co.		Minneapolis, Minnesota
Jopp Electric		Princeton, Minnesota
Lejay		Minneapolis, Minnesota
McColly		Hinsdale, Montana
Nelson Electric	Allied Electric	Spencer, Iowa
Parker-McCrory		Kansas City, Missouri
Parris-Dunn	Dunn Manufacturing	Clarinda, Iowa
Pioneer		Chicago, Illinois
Ruralite		Sioux City, Iowa
Universal Battery Co.	HEBCO / Perkins Electric	Chicago, Illinois
White		Wichita, Kansas
Wind Motor		Ridgeway, Montana
Wincharger Corp.	Albers Propellor Co. / Winco	Sioux City, Iowa
Wind Power Light Co.	Miller Airlite / Winpower	Newton, Iowa

Chapter 6

SELLING ELECTRICITY

Thomas Edison's vision of an electric power plant that could sell electricity to everyone within a mile

Up to this point, I have focused on the significant devices associated with electricity and the migration of this equipment into commercialization and service. At the turn of the last century, a new force came into play that had little to do with technology and everything to do with the development of the business model that would come to dominate and ultimately give us the electric supply system of today. This model started with Thomas Edison's idea of "selling" electricity.

As we have seen, the commercialization of electricity began with the manufacture and sale of equipment to industry, commerce, and municipalities. This would ultimately migrate to rural and remote homes and businesses beginning with the Delco-Light plant. Industry investors were focused and intent on making money manufacturing and selling electrical equipment. Edison championed a different concept of selling electricity. Since he had developed all the elements of a complete electric system, from generators to light bulbs, he wanted to supply it all and get the income from both the electricity and light bulbs, which at that time burned out in about 20 minutes. In the beginning, he sold the entire system primarily to municipalities for street lighting and did so with a fair degree of success. With the Edison system, a single

power plant only served an area within one mile. This was due to the fact that his system was direct current and operated at a fixed 110 volts.

Nikola Tesla, an eccentric scientist and visionary who once worked for Edison but abruptly quit when Edison reneged on a financial commitment, would go on to develop an alternating current system that was far superior to Edison's for generating, transmitting, and distributing electricity. The Tesla alternating current system could generate electricity at a higher voltage, increase the voltage using a transformer developed by Tesla himself, and transmit it efficiently over long distances. Transformers at substations would lower the voltage for distributing the electricity locally. A final service transformer near each home would reduce the voltage again for delivery to the meter for use by the electric customer, typically 120-volts alternating current as today in its most common form. A single distant large power plant could supply electricity to much larger areas which was more economical, and so the "economy of scale" argument was born. Tesla teamed up with industrialist George Westinghouse to compete vigorously with Edison in selling entire electric systems to cities. First demonstrated at the Chicago World's Fair in 1893 (World's Columbian Exposition) with 250,000

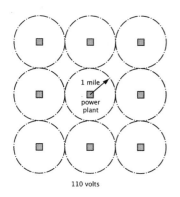

1 mile
power
plant

110 volts

Direct current system

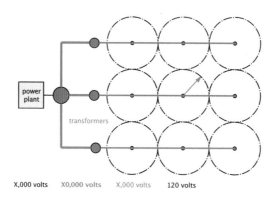

power
plant

transformers

X,000 volts   X0,000 volts   X,000 volts   120 volts

Alternating current system

Nikola Tesla and George Westinghouse envisioned a system where a single large power plant with transformers could serve everyone within several miles.

light bulbs, the Tesla and Westinghouse alternating current system would soon be chosen for the power plant at Niagara Falls. It would supply power to Buffalo, 20 miles away, which was simply not practical for Edison's 110 volt direct current system. Tesla went on to make advances in motor technology, fluorescent and neon lightning, wireless communication (including radio, radar and Doppler radar) and presented ideas in an endless stream including some that have yet to be proven but remain a scientific curiosity. The Westinghouse alternating current system prevailed and Edison ultimately converted and changed the name from Edison Electric Works to General Electric in the process. Large power generating plants with step-up transformers would come to dominate the landscape, especially near water resources.

Although Edison had the initial idea of selling electricity, one of his aides, Samuel Insull, would have a far greater impact on our modern central station-dominated supply network. This lesser known person in his time would become one of the most powerful men in the United States. Insull cashed out when Edison became General Electric and accepted a job in 1892 as president of Chicago Edison Co., a small lighting company that had previously purchased Edison equipment. He started another electric company, Commonwealth Light and Power, a few years later and the two became Commonwealth Edison in 1907. Insull acquired and merged it into a web of electric generating capability, including electric railroads, to become a modern-day giant serving metropolitan Chicago and major portions of the Midwest. His company also evolved into an important force in the national grid. Within 40 years, Insull became the president of 11 major power companies, chairman of 65, and director of 85, when his entire empire collapsed in 1932, completely wiping out his 600,000

investors. It seems as though his trusts and holding companies were highly leveraged to the point of defying reason. His life's work, however, inspired two accomplishments, one literary, Citizen Kane, and the other legislative, the Public Utility Holding Company Act, which passed Congress in 1935 to "regulate" such risky behavior. Insull fled the country to avoid fraud prosecution but was extradited, tried, and found not guilty in the end. He retired to France, and died in Paris on Bastille Day. He was buried in London, the city of his birth.

Insull's legacy is more compelling. From his earliest days in Chicago, he was devoted to promoting and establishing the principles used to justify the "natural monopoly" status of the electric power companies and incredibly argued for regulation. In the early 1900s, it was common for private interests to purchase municipal electric utilities, an idea that provoked skepticism about the lack of market competition and thus potential for an unnatural advantage subject to abuse.

Regardless, it was the rage at the time and Insull's ways inspired others to follow. By 1921, 91 percent of all the electric utilities in the United States were privately owned. New York investors were so impressed that they bought and "consolidated" 29 local electric companies into one, forming Consolidated Edison, or "Con Ed" as it has become known. The process would lead to the dominant business model for our present day electric supplier network.

The principles used to accomplish this were based on two basic axioms that have served as the foundation for shaping the argument for a natural monopoly and the network into its present state. An axiom is generally a "recognized truth" or an "established and universally accepted principle or rule." In a more disciplined scientific definition, an axiom

Large electric power plants with step-up transformers near large bodies of cooling water would come to dominate.

is "a proposition which is presumed without proof for the sake of studying the consequences that follow from it." I'm inclined to believe that the science definition serves us better, especially as it relates to the part about "without proof" and "consequences that follow." So let's analyze the axioms, proofs, and consequences.

Axiom 1

Electricity cannot be stored. It must be generated, transmitted, and used in the very same instant.

Proof

There is no proof whatsoever. In fact, without electricity stored in the primary and secondary battery, it is quite possible that Faraday and other inventors would not have advanced electric technology at the pace that they did, if at all. It is also clear that both the electric power and communications industries would have advanced much more slowly as a result. Electric battery technology became commercially popular and found its way into our daily lives in increasing measure throughout history and with significant benefits. Furthermore, other means of storing electricity, namely pumped hydro storage, have become a popular way for electric power companies to improve their efficiency and provide high value-added capacity. It was false, and Insull knew it. In fact, he had major investments in storage batteries for his system to insure the continuity of service as they were more reliable than the steam generators.

Consequences

The truthfulness of this served as the foundation of the second axiom with the consequences being to establish a century-long pattern of building increasingly larger, and more expensive power plants. It also destroyed the farm electric plant industry and was the primary reason that solar, wind, and biofuel technology advancement has been stifled and held irrelevant for the past 90 years.

Axiom 2

Power plants are very expensive to build.

Proof

In a limited and conditional sense this is true. The expense is proportional to the size and inversely proportional to the efficiency. Large power plants that are complex and inefficient are indeed very expensive to build.

Consequences

Insull used these "truths" to put forth the proposition that electric companies were a natural monopoly to justify his acquisitions of all the private, public, transit, and municipal generating systems in the region. Furthermore, in a classic "please don't throw me in that briar patch" plea, he sought and got public regulation of a private "investor-owned" electric utility monopoly. In the compromise with the opposition, he convinced them that public regulation would prohibit taking advantage of the monopoly status by regulating the prices an electric utility could charge to avoid excess. He did this based on his experience with the railroads (He would come to own a few of them, too). The "regulators" would by law have to set rates at a level to ensure a "fair" rate of return on the huge investments in power plants. Economists have come to refer to this derisively as a "lazy monopoly." In summary, no competition or risk allowed investor-owned electric utilities to dominate the capital markets and encouraged them to make investments in increasingly larger and grossly inefficient power plants. I fail to understand how this reconciles with the principles of free enterprise capitalism. The consequence was the domination of a handful of regional private utilities operating a national electrical network with excess overcapacity and an antiquated and inefficient conversion system of generation, transmission, and distribution networks. It should have been obvious that by eliminating risk, the electric companies would invest as much as possible, regardless of the temerity of the investment, and the financial markets would give them all the capital they asked for. We will return to the matter of examining our resulting national electric supply network and efficiency in a subsequent chapter.

When Insull took control of the Chicago Edison Co., the electric industry business operated on the J. P. Morgan model of selling equipment to private industry, public transportation, municipal lighting, and private businesses. His competitors were the companies and municipalities that Edison and Westinghouse had fought vigorously over for the past several years, and they owned generating equipment. Axioms in hand, he set out to convince others. His argument began with a tale about a north side Chicago neighborhood of 193 households, of which 189 were his customers. At this point, lights were the primary use for electricity since all of the other common appliances that we use today were simply not available at the time. If each house had a generator, the total capacity would have to be 68.5 kilowatts to operate the lights. Insull pointed out that since each home would turn on lamps at different times, the maximum at any time would be far less, about 20 kilowatts. Since electricity could not be stored, it follows that one 20-kilowatt generator serving everyone would be far better than everyone having their own generator which would total 68.5 kilowatts. So what is the point when nearly all of the homes are your customers? Well the fact that his home customers only used electricity during a few hours in the morning and evening for lighting meant that other customers

could be served at other times. When people left their homes in the morning and turned their lights off, they got on a street car for the ride to work and the reverse was true at the end of the work day. When they were not at home or on the public transit, they were either working or sleeping. The next step was for Insull to secure the contract to supply electricity to the streetcar companies because power plants were expensive to build, electricity could not be stored, and he could supply the railroads with 17 percent less capacity - and thus lower cost. Street cars required large amounts of electricity and were the largest consumers of electricity at the time.

Street car companies typically owned their own generating plants. It was not uncommon at the time for large industrial companies to own power plants for their operations. Match this with Insull's spare capacity during mid-day and overnight, and I bet he would practically give the electricity to industrial users so they would stop building their own power plants. By charging homes nearly 25 times as much for a unit of electricity, he was able to sell electricity to industrial customers for a little less than the cost they would pay for just the fuel if they built their own power plant. Business and commercial customers would, of course, be entitled to pay a little less than homeowners, too.

This same structure exists today. Homes pay more, while businesses pay less, and industry pays the least per unit of electricity. Investor-owned electric utilities operate 75 percent of the generating capacity that supplies 75 percent of the electric customers. In 1998, there were 3,170 "traditional" electric utilities in the United States contributing to our nation's electric capacity.

- 239 investor-owned with 75 percent of the generating capacity.

- 2,009 publicly-owned with 10 percent of the generating capacity.

- 912 consumer-owned/rural electric cooperatives with 4 percent of the generating capacity.

- 10 federal electric utilities with 10 percent of the generating capacity.

Virtually all of the electricity produced today uses the steam cycle and is a very complicated and subsequently inefficient way to convert fuel energy. This is especially true when the energy cost of mining

The New York Railway's 6th Street plant under construction with 20,000-horsepower steam turbines

An artist's drawing of a modern nuclear power plant in a peaceful, secluded setting

Inside the powerhouse, steam turbines drive the generators continuously.

A central station power plant promotional ad conveniently omits the piles of coal, cooling system, and exhaust gases.

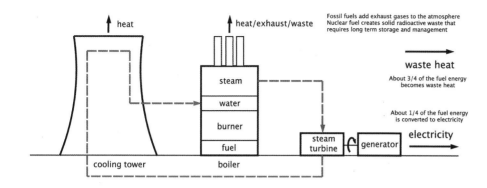

A typical steam power plant with boiler, steam turbine, generator, and cooling tower to condense the steam into water

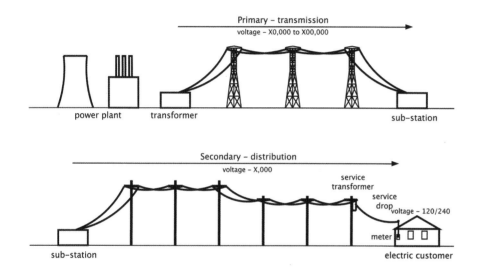

High voltage is transmitted from the power plant to substations which lower the voltage for local distribution to a service transformer which lowers the voltage for use.

the fuel, and in the case of uranium the added cost of enrichment subsidies, are considered.

The only exception is the federal dams which convert potential energy directly to electricity. The steam cycle burns fuel to heat water and produces steam, which spins a turbine and in turn a generator to produce electricity. The steam is cooled and returned as water to begin the process over again. The problem is that for each unit of electric energy produced for consumption, it requires four units of energy be "burned" and three units of energy placed in the atmosphere as wasted heat. In addition to the heat, the combustion exhaust gases and solid radioactive nuclear wastes are a product of this process.

Once converted, electricity is transformed and transmitted over primary long distance lines before being transformed and distributed over secondary regional lines and transformed again for service to the electric customer. This entire process involves additional losses of energy at each step of the way. The power lines in rural areas have a disproportionately large amount of losses.

By contrast, hydroelectric power, primarily from the federal dams, converts the potential (height) energy of the water directly to electricity with any unused energy converted to kinetic (motion) energy, which powers, along with gravity, the flow of the water to its natural level. There is absolutely no wasted heat placed into the atmosphere, and no exhaust gases or solid waste.

The same is true for both solar and wind energy. A final important point, with solar panels on your roof or a wind plant in your yard, there are no transmission and distribution losses. Each unit of electricity you generate eliminates the need to burn four-times the amount of fuel energy from somewhere else. I think we are on to something if we could only "store" electricity.

The success of Commonwealth Edison inspired other metropolitan areas and regions to do the same, such as Consolidated Edison, Baltimore Gas and Electric, Duke Power, American Electric Power, Detroit Edison, Southern Companies, Florida Power and Light and dozens more familiar names. Each entity, powerful in its own right, was convinced to

Large transformers are used to increase or decrease voltage between the power plant and electric customer.

High voltage transmission lines carry power long distances between cities and have become interconnected from coast to coast.

join together in an industry trade organization, the Edison Electric Institute, to increase their power and promote the use of electricity. Since profits, in absolute terms, were guaranteed and determined by the cost of generating equipment, which was determined by the size and inefficiency of each power plant, the pathway to maximum profitability was to increase demand. In addition to encouraging industrial inefficiency and waste through favorable rate structures, the best way to increase demand in homes was to promote electricity for space and water heating. Space and water heating use the most energy in a home and electricity is the least efficient way to provide them. For nearly 40 years, the all-electric home was promoted vigorously, primarily to builders who installed electric heating equipment for much less, not counting the promotional incentives, with the cost difference going directly to profits and not to lower home costs. The customer would, of course, ultimately have to pay two- to three- times more for electricity than they would for natural gas, propane, or even fuel oil each month thereafter. This is another major mistake that has a disproportionately negative effect on our energy delivery system and should be corrected in a smart, easy, and rational way to improve our network efficiency. We will come back to this matter also.

As we will see, the result is an electric system with a vast amount of unnecessary capacity, fueled by investment without risk and reason. By 2006 in the United States, the peak summer demand was 789,475 megawatts and the peak winter demand was 640,981 megawatts. The U.S. net summer generating capacity was 986,125 megawatts, or 25 percent extra capacity in summer, 54 percent extra capacity in winter, and even more in spring and fall. The overall conversion efficiency for electricity generation, transmission, and distribution from all energy sources, including hydro power, was about 31 percent. Since hydro plants do not put out any waste heat, the overall efficiency for the steam power plants falls to 26% when the dams are removed from consideration. This means that 75 percent of the energy in coal, gas, oil, and nuclear goes into the atmosphere as wasted heat.

This same year, the average cost of each unit, or kilowatt-hour of electricity, was 8.9 cents. Residential customers used 37 percent of the electricity and paid 10.4 cents; commercial customers used 35 percent

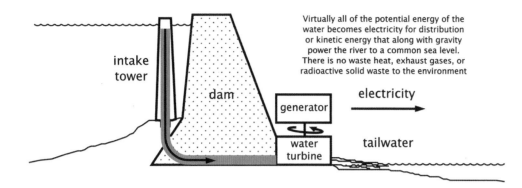

Virtually all of the potential energy of the water becomes electricity for distribution or kinetic energy that along with gravity power the river to a common sea level. There is no waste heat, exhaust gases, or radioactive solid waste to the environment

intake tower

dam

generator

electricity

water turbine

tailwater

A hydroelectric plant uses the potential energy of the water to turn the generators to produce electricity without waste.

and paid 9.5 cents; and industrial customers used 28 percent and paid 6.2 cents. Residential electricity usage fell by 0.6 percent in 2005, which is only second time that has happened since 1974.

As you will note above, the federal generating capacity is about 10 percent and grew simultaneously with the investor-owned and municipal electric utilities. Along with the capacity increases, the federal government expanded a host of other interconnected activities that would include regulation, research and development, preferential uses, and "promotional" activities. As a result, only 10 percent of the federal generation is provided to the retail market and 90 percent to preferred customers at cost with no profit. The federal capacity represents another significant portion of our present day supply network and is worth understanding better.

In the 1990s, the electric utility industry got caught up in the privatization and de-regulation frenzy that resulted in the rise and fall of the Enron business model, harkening back to the days of Samuel Insull and the collapse of his empire in the early 1930s. The historical regulatory relationships between the "natural monopolies" and their regulatory partners have been dramatically altered in the process. In the past few years, the energy and electric utility industries have been neglected and require public attention and scrutiny. Any future improvements to our electric supply network will require a fresh look at the role of private and public interests, in addition to the establishment of policy and practices that best serve the citizens and businesses, to meet market demands and improve the lives of consumers.

The generators in this powerhouse are located above the water wheels and produce pure electricity.

Chapter 7

GIVING ELECTRICITY

Theodore Roosevelt Dam on the Salt River

With all the excitement of electricity that marked the late 1800s, it was a given that the federal government could not stay on the sidelines for long. The expanding popularity of water powered electric systems just seemed like a natural starting place to get involved.

In 1881, a Grand Rapids, Michigan hydro plant powered a string of 16 arc lights, and the following year the first Edison 110-volt power plant in Appleton, Wisconsin began operation. Five years later, the number of hydropower plants grew to more than 50 and would quadruple within three years. In 1895, the Westinghouse alternating current power plant at Niagara Falls started supplying electricity to Buffalo 20 miles away.

From small beginnings, starting with the Federal Water Power Act of 1902 establishing federal authority over the nation's waterways and creating the Bureau of Reclamation the following year, the federal government would become a major player in the electric supply network. By the end of World War II, federal dams produced 40 percent of the nation's electric supply. The percentage dropped to its present level of about 6.5 percent over the next 60 years. The hydropower path and the evolving federal involvement in electric power is an interesting study and worth understanding.

The first project for the Bureau of Reclamation was the Theodore Roosevelt Dam on the Salt River, about 50 miles east of Phoenix, Arizona. Made of masonry blocks, the dam began operation supplying power to Phoenix and irrigation for the surrounding arid farms. It became very popular with local citizens. The dam was financed federally by using 200,000 acres committed by local citizens to serve as collateral. Today it is the third largest public utility in the country and serves central Arizona, operating five hydropower plants and three steam plants, and participating in cooperative generating ventures. The board is elected on a "debt proportion" basis by local landowners, one vote per acre, according to the original financing provisions of 1903.

The Bureau of Reclamation, operating in the 17 western states, would build the Hoover Dam, Grand Coulee Dam, and the California Central Valley Project. It managed the water resources to provide irrigation and electricity, and ultimately operated 58 power plants. The bureau's electric business today is managed by four federal marketing administrations: Bonneville, Southeastern, Southwestern, and Western. The bureau is also the largest wholesale source of water in the United States.

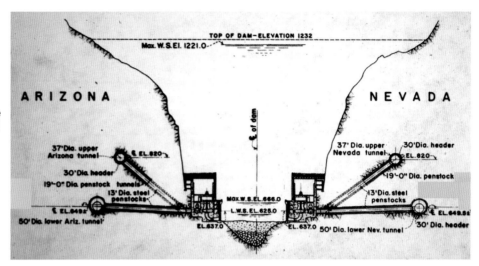

Hoover Dam, originally Boulder Dam, bridges the gap between Arizona and Nevada to harness the energy of the Colorado River.

The Wilson Dam at Muscle Shoals, Alabama, was completed in 1927.

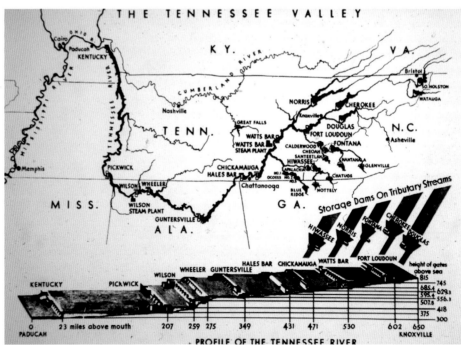

The Tennessee Valley Authority plan for the Tennessee River watershed spanned seven states.

The National Defense Act of 1917 further tight-ened federal control of all waterways and authorized the Army Corps of Engineers to construct the Wilson Dam at Muscle Shoals, Alabama. Started in 1918 and completed in 1927, the 645-megawatt dam became part of the yet to be established Tennessee Valley Authority in 1933. The Army Corps of Engineers, which demonstrated its capabilities during the Civil War and with the construction of railroads and the Panama Canal, was an obvious choice for managing the nation's dams, rivers, and flood control programs. In addition to the waterways, the Corps of Engineers became the largest public construction engineering organization, with responsibility for design and con-struction of Army, Air Force, and national defense facilities.

Meanwhile, the Federal Power Act of 1920 es-tablished the Federal Power Commission, made up of the secretaries of war, interior, and agriculture, to stimulate water-power development with "authority over all matters pertaining to the water power de-velopment along, from, or in navigable waters of the U.S.," including public lands, Indian reservations, and territories. As time went by, the commission's power expanded to the electric supply and electric and gas transmission, including regulating the affairs of the industry. In 1930, control of the FPC was turned over to an independent commission with commissioners appointed by the president with the Senate's consent. The era of federal involvement in the electric supply network was about to increase significantly.

In 1933, the Tennessee Valley Authority was established with an aggressive plan to manage the regional watershed. It grew with time to become the largest of the three federal agencies operating power generation facilities and surpassing the two other federal agencies created earlier, the Corps of Engineers and the Bureau of Reclamation. All of these agencies have primary portfolio holdings in our national dams but with time have expanded into electrical generation with other fuels.

Envisioned as a means to counteract the excess-es of the investor-owned utility monopolies, trusts, and holding companies that contributed to the Great Depression and to re-establish public participation in the electric industry, the TVA started with lofty goals. It tamed the ravages of winter rains in the Tennes-see River watershed, an area involving all or part of seven states, provided a navigable waterway for commerce, generated clean electric power for the region to improve the lives of people and subsidize regional industries, created jobs by the thousands,

The generators and water turbines below them are a testament to the engineering excellence and flawless performance of the Tennessee Valley Authority dams.

boosted an entire region economically, and served as a model for developing public electric power in every other watershed in the country.

It did achieve most of these goals with the excep-tion of the last one. Privately owned electric utilities despised this effort. Wendell Willkie, president of Commonwealth & Southern Company, a Samuel Insull company (now the Southern Company and a major regional electric utility), fought bitterly against the TVA and lost. He was forced to sell C&S facili-ties in the area to the TVA. He gained the Republi-can nomination for president in 1940 to run against

Franklin Roosevelt's New Deal policies and was handily defeated. The competition between private and public power continues to generate controversy and has become an ongoing and inextricable part of the electric supply network.

It was a remarkable engineering achievement and a testimony to the TVA Chairman Arthur Morgan to develop a system of 35 high and low dams for river traffic and electric power that has operated flawlessly ever since. The program began in earnest. Five thousand jobs were created in just five weeks by the new Roosevelt administration, and tens of thousands of good jobs would soon follow. Fifteen thousand families had to be relocated from the 300,000 acres to be permanently flooded by the headwaters. Morgan's vision went beyond the dams to affecting the

Rural Electrification Administration

The Rural Electrification Act of 1936 created the Rural Electrification Administration.

Rural Electrification Administration guidelines required at least two customers per mile, but were frequently ignored.

surrounding communities. He developed a model city, Norris, Tennessee, for workers and families that was wholesome and different from "stereotypical construction shanty towns." Good schools; successful businesses; clean, efficient homes with modern conveniences; hospitals and health care; and libraries with book mobiles were all part of it.

The TVA did contribute to the well-being of the region and the engineering legacy is quite remark-

able. In a highly public dispute over social and economic issues with his controversial TVA Director David Lilienthal, Morgan was fired by President Roosevelt in 1938. Lilienthal was put in charge until 1946 and changed the direction of the agency. He went on to become the first chairman of the U. S. Atomic Energy Commission. The TVA's generating system today consists of 29 dams, 11 coal plants, 83 combustion turbines, and three nuclear plants.

Over the years, a great deal of TVA power has been diverted to "preferred" customers, such as energy-intensive aluminum production, uranium enrichment for weapons and electricity, and the rural electric cooperatives. Today, only 10 percent of the TVA's energy is supplied to retail customers.

In a monumental act of irrationality, justifiable only by a lack of knowledge or understanding, the federal government decided to do what no investor-owned utility would even begin to consider doing, extending the central station wires from the major urban centers to every rural and remote part of the nation. In fact, the electric utilities resisted the idea at first but eventually acquiesced, accepted the increased demand, and "invested" in large new power plants. The Rural Electrification Administration was established as an "emergency" agency by executive order of President Roosevelt in May 1935 "to carry electricity to as many farms as possible in the shortest possible time and to have it used in quantities sufficient to affect rural life." It was transformed into a permanent agency by the Rural Electrification Act of 1936 which provided federal funding to install the electric transmission and distribution lines to rural areas. Member-owned rural cooperatives were established to purchase power wholesale for distribution over their own network of transmission and distribution lines.

This was justified by the "unavailability of electricity in farms, ranches, and remote places." In 1926, the electric utilities provided service to about 310,000 farms, usually close to cities, with electric power. An even greater number of farms, typically farther from the city, were served by a Delco-Light electric plant. An even greater number emerges when the sales of the other farm electric plant companies are included in the total. These numbers continued to grow, even during the early years of the depression, and the "new" wind generator sales began growing to add to this total. The farm electric plants were not even considered in the discussion.

The long distances involved with supplying rural power lines was an order of magnitude greater than urban areas. To make matters worse, the 2,300-volt distribution used in the cities was not practical and a 6,900-volt system was required, which was far more expensive for the wires and service transformers. Furthermore, the power losses per customer were far greater. The wires were more vulnerable to severe weather resulting in frequent outages, and the rural distribution lines were much more expensive to maintain and repair after strong storms given the distances involved.

The Rural Electrification Administration (REA) pushed forward relentlessly, and it was a favorite voter carrot for politicians. The member-owned rural cooperatives vigorously built their transmission and distribution lines sometimes with a little helpful congressional "oversight." Some farm homes that had their own electric plant prohibited their neighbors from getting electricity, resulting in not enough customers per mile to meet federal guidelines. So, a little neighborly persuasion was used to get them off their Delco-Light plants and onto the "high line." This included changing all of the wiring and replacing all of their 32-volt appliances. The REA required wind and farm electric systems be removed or destroyed before the agency allowed them to connect. In exchange, each customer got a 230-volt, 60-amp service. It included a 60-amp electric range circuit, a 20-amp kitchen circuit, and two or three lighting circuits for ceiling mounted lights, with a switch at the entry to the room.

In 1939, the congressional record bragged that $210 million was spent to install nearly 100,000 miles of lines to provide electricity to nearly 220,000 homes. The national average of 2.2 homes per mile at $2,100 per mile means that a little over $950 per home was spent. For that same amount of money, a Jacobs wind generator, 50 foot tower, large 440 ampere-hour battery, and a new 1,500-watt Delco-Light could have been installed at each home with enough left over for a well pump, a full compliment of household appliances, and an efficient "bottled gas" tank for heating and cooking. I think the farms would have been served far better with the farm light plant. During the same three-year period, the electric utilities began serving 20 percent more farms than the REA as they increased their service to more of the farms surrounding the cities.

With respect to "affecting rural life," I'm not sure that during the ensuing years the effect on rural communities was positive overall. The argument could be made that the power lines that brought electricity to rural America carried away rural money to far away places and that over the past 80 years the family farm, rural businesses and industry, and farm communities frequently suffered more than gained from the lofty ideals originally conceived.

This policy and program was one of the most significant mistakes made in the development of our electric supply network. At the center of any future national energy policy, the dismantling of this network and the reintroduction of private wind, solar, genset, battery hybrid power systems for country homes,

Completed in 1941, the
Grand Coulee Dam on
the Columbia River is the
largest U. S. dam and the
fifth largest in the world.
*Source: U.S. Geological
Survey, Washington, D.C.*

Completed in 1937, the
Bonneville Dam provides
electricity and river
navigation just east of
Portland, Oregon.

Detroit Edison's Enrico
Fermi 1 fast breeder
reactor would have been
spared responsibility had
it "actually" melted down
in 1966 before losing its
operating license.

farms, and communities using local energy sources would have the greatest overall effect on the efficiency, reasonableness, and quality of our national electric delivery system. Transferring portions of this technology to urban areas could compound the benefits. We will examine the impact of doing this.

The Bureau of Reclamation and Corps of Engineers were not sitting idly by during this period. In 1933 President Roosevelt authorized construction of the Grand Coulee Dam, the largest U.S. dam, as a Works Progress Administration project to manage the water and energy resources of the Columbia and Snake rivers in the Pacific Northwest. An additional 31 dams were built along these two rivers, significantly contributing to the nation's electric supply. In the early 1940s, dams accounted for nearly 40 percent of the nation's electric supply, and power lines were going up all across the country.

The Bonneville Dam led to the Bonneville Power Administration which became the model federal power marketing agency to give electricity away to preferred customers at cost.

World War II had a profound and lasting impact on our nation's involvement with energy and electricity. The day after my first birthday, the atomic bomb was dropped on Hiroshima and the ending of the war took on new dimensions. The top secret Manhattan Project that created the weapon was a monumental task, which involved 130,000 highly skilled scientists working at the national laboratories of Oak Ridge, Hanford, Los Alamos, Berkeley, Ames, Argonne, and other familiar names, some that could not be mentioned at the time, doing things they could not talk about. Interestingly, Oak Ridge and Hanford were assigned the task of enriching uranium, an extremely energy-intensive process, using as much as 10% of the nation's electric output at times. It was no accident that these facilities were built close the Tennessee River and Columbia River for access as a "preferred" customer to incredibly cheap hydroelectric power from the dams.

On August 1, 1946, four days before my second birthday, President Truman signed the Atomic Energy Act into law. The law ruled that nuclear weapon development and nuclear energy management would be under civilian rather than military control and established the U.S. Atomic Energy Commission, primarily from the laboratories of the Manhattan Project. David Lilienthal of TVA fame was named the first chairman to the commission and he would lead the new organization with the dual task of promoting and regulating nuclear technology, which would prove impossible.

The peaceful atom program was off and running. The power of the atom would produce limitless electricity and cure diseases like cancer with extremely carcinogenic ionizing radiation from radioactive nuclear fission byproducts. Children at the time had their feet X-rayed to "see" if shoes fit and read comic books distributed in schools about the wonder of the atom while being rained on by ionizing radiation from the hundreds of atomic bomb tests conducted in the atmosphere before the Limited Test Ban Treaty was signed in 1963 by some countries and even adhered to by a few. Nuclear power was so desirable and so safe Congress passed the Price-Anderson Act in 1957 to indemnify power companies against liability claims from nuclear "incidents."

By the late 1960s, the Atomic Energy Commission had the nuclear promotion pedal to the floor with unrealistic plans to build between 450 and 650 nuclear power plants before the end of the century and the foot off the regulatory brake. That, combined with an unwillingness to look for health risks associated with radiation and an ongoing national debate about safe levels, resulted in a loss of confidence that doomed the organization. In 1975, the Atomic Energy Commission was broken into the Energy Research and Development Administration (ERDA) and the Nuclear Regulatory Commission with single purpose tasks. The sale of nuclear power plants stopped abruptly and did not pick up, despite many expensive and ineffective efforts to do so. Two years later, ERDA combined with the Federal Energy Administration to become the Department of Energy. Although the Department of Energy branched out to many areas, nuclear weapons and energy programs have continued to be a primary focus and responsibility. During the ERDA years and the Carter administration, an openness to renewable energy technology, specifically wind and solar, was briefly embraced after the oil crisis. At this same time, a creative group of engineers at Windworks developed the Gemini Synchronous Inverter, an electronic device that permitted variable output direct current electrical sources, such as solar panels and wind generators, to connect to electric utility networks in a shared manner.

When the solar production exceeded the household demand, the excess went back into the electric network for use by other electric customers. When the household demand exceeded solar production, the utility supplied the difference. As a representative

The innovative Gemini synchronous inverter connected private wind generators and solar panels to the electric network.

The Windworker 10 (10 meters and 10 kilowatt), which was developed with federal support, provided more than enough power for an average home.

of the fledgling American Wind Energy Association, I was able to successfully argue for and obtain federal support for small wind energy conversion systems. A few of these projects were very successful in advancing small wind energy technology, increasing performance knowledge, and gaining operational experience. Many of the small solar electric projects and wind generators developed for these programs were used in grid-intertie projects via the Gemini and other similar equipment. The openness to wind and solar electricity slowly waned in the early 1980s along with falling oil prices and the new Reagan administration's lack of interest in wind and solar power.

In 1978, Congress passed the Public Utility Regulatory Policies Act (PURPA) to encourage renewable energy and non-utility participation in supplying electricity. It essentially opened the network to non-utility electric producers, such as homeowners like me with a windmill at the time, to large industrial plants with their own generating equipment. Of course the terms were helped along by electric industry lobbyists to favor the electric companies and discourage small producers. The argument was that the only benefit to the electric utility for allowing small private power producers to participate in their network was to avoid the generating investment cost, which was about 20 percent of the total cost. Therefore, it seemed fair to them that they would buy electricity for 20 percent of what they sold it for. The concern about return on investment for the truly private investor, who chose to produce electricity by purchasing equipment in the marketplace, was not apparent in the utilities' definition of free enterprise capitalism.

In 1975, I installed the first wind generator in the country to supply power to a private residence by connecting to the electric network in Ann Arbor, Michigan. The local utility, Detroit Edison, reluctantly agreed to permit me to connect, under threat of imminent national public exposure, and sheepishly put forward a service agreement where they would install two directional meters and pay me 20 percent of what they would charge for the energy. It was totally ridiculous for two reasons. The first was that the wind generator was an antique Jacobs Wind Electric designed in the 1920s operating in modest southern Michigan winds supplying power to a residence belonging to a large family with above average energy usage. It was admittedly unlikely that any net electricity would be produced for Detroit Edison to buy so there would be no expense for them. Secondly, they didn't want to set a bad precedent of a homeowner producing electricity. Who knows what the impact of tens of thousands of homeowners, businesses, and industries producing electricity would have been on the utility?

Some utilities became more progressive and fair in their policies for independent power producers. A few years after my Ann Arbor installation, I put up another Jacobs wind generator and connected it to my home electric panel. Wisconsin Electric, to its credit, gave me a "net energy billing" contract, which paid equally for the power bought and sold. I congratulate and thank them for their vision and fairness. In this case, the winds in Wisconsin were a little higher and my usage was below average. In the 20 months that I operated this system I produced more power than I used. In fact, I produced enough extra power to overcome my monthly service fees and received a check from Wisconsin Electric for 97 cents when I closed my account and moved. Undaunted by the electric utility's resistance, in 2001, there were 2,110

non-utility power producers supplying electricity to the network. Although they account for a very small portion of the national capacity, there is a great deal of future potential for homeowners, businesses, and industrial facilities to play a major role in the production of electricity with an open network.

Today, the federal public electric contribution to our national electric supply is about 10 percent from 180 generating facilities, primarily dams. Most of the electricity is still devoted to rural electric cooperatives and preferred customers. The electricity produced is sold at cost which is well below the national average. The government has staked out a position in the electric network and is a force to be considered moving forward. Hopefully, future involvement will build on the positive accomplishments and policies, move away from policies that were misguided, and contribute overall to the growth of solar and wind technologies and private investment in generation.

My wind-powered home in Wisconsin

Chapter 8

USING ELECTRICITY

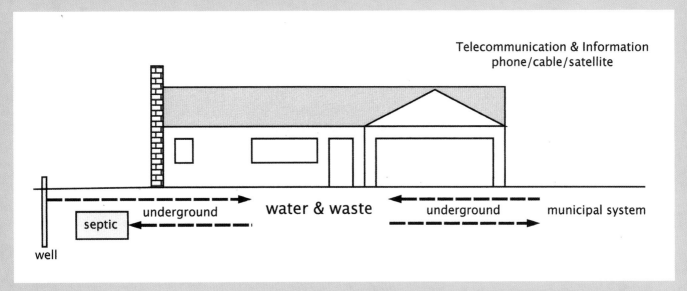

Telecommunication & Information
phone/cable/satellite

water & waste

underground   underground   municipal system

septic

well

Water and waste management is typically supplied by a municipal water utility in the city or by the homeowner in the form of a well and septic system in the country.

A rational approach to fulfilling our wishes, wants, and needs begins with determining what they are and how best to meet them. For our purposes, we will start with a typical family home. The process can be adapted to retail, commercial, and industrial levels and even be applied to a community, village, town, or city composed of all of these elements.

It is important to understand the relationship of energy in general and electricity specifically to our lives if we are going to find better means to meet our needs. Electricity is one of five essential common interest services, categorized as utilities, which serve homes, businesses, and industry. The other four are water, sewer, thermal, and telecommunications. In a general sense, a supply of clean water, a means of dealing with sanitary waste, a source of thermal energy for warmth, electricity for general use, and telecommunications are essential services that a normal modern family rely on. For our purposes, we will focus on the water, waste, thermal, and electrical needs as they all involve power in some respect and may be interconnected depending on where you live.

Water and Waste

Every home has an essential need for water and for dealing with liquid waste or sewerage. A clean supply of water, what we use it for, and how we obtain it is a good starting point. In the United States, 34 percent of our water is from ground water and 66 percent is from surface water. Water is generally used for drinking, bathing, food preparation, washing clothes and dishes, and waste purposes inside the home but can also be used for lawns, gardens, livestock, and other purposes outside the home. In cities and small towns, the common need for water and sewer services brings citizens together in every community to form a municipal water and sewer "utility" through a regional or local government or cooperative of some sort. Frequently referred to as "city water," all the water supplied to each home has been filtered and treated chemically and is suitable for human consumption - potable water. It should be noted that only a small percentage of a home's water usage is used for drinking. From a central source, such as a deep well, river, or lake, the utility pumps the water and maintains pressure to an underground network of water lines, buried deep enough to prevent freezing, to each home and business in the community being served.

Sanitary waste is the output of the water supply system in all its forms and is equally important to consider, given the health implications of not dealing with this matter wisely. Normally, in areas with a public water utility, sanitary waste is also provided in the form of sewer or "return" pipes buried underground that return the home waste water to a sanitary treatment and filtration plant before returning to the environment. In the United States, about three quarters of the homes are connected to a public sewer treatment system. Municipal bonds finance the underground lines, and fees charged to users for water and sewer services are used to retire the debt, cover operating and maintenance expenses, and hopefully have a little left over to plan for future expansion and service improvements. The energy to pump the water and process the waste is an operating expense for the municipal water utility, and the costs are included in the service fee. On a national basis, about 3 percent of the electricity we generate is used for water and sewer services. In the United States, 74 percent of our water is supplied by utilities that are publicly-owned and 11 percent by those that are investor-owned. The remaining 15 percent have wells, primarily country homes and rural farms. Although there are 605 major water and waste utilities, there are over 53,000 water systems in the United States. The vast majority of these water systems serve cities with less than 4,000 homes.

For homes beyond the reach of the public water utilities, a well is generally drilled close to the home and an electrical well motor is used to pump water to the home. In some areas, where the water table is within 30 feet of the surface (generally in low lying areas or areas close to natural water sources, such as streams, ponds, or lakes) a shallow well pump is used and a motor mounted on top of the well drives a pump that "pulls" the water up. The more common form of well pump, which can work in very deep wells, is the submersible pump/motor that is lowered to the bottom of the well casing and "pushes" the water up. In either case, the well pump turns on when the pressure in a pressure tank drops to a preset low level as water is used. It runs until the high pressure limit is reached when the pressure tank is full. Take a shower, wash a load of clothes, or flush the toilet several times and the pump will run for a few minutes until the water is replaced, the pressure rises, and the pump turns off. Well water may, and usually does, require filtering, softening, and/or a means to insure that it is safe for consumption. In the first case, electricity is used by the water utility to pump water to all the homes that it serves. For the rural home, the homeowner's electric service provides the power to pump the water into the home. In most cases the amount of power for the well pump in a single family home is generally small, about 5 percent of basic electrical energy. The importance of maintaining clean running water, however, cannot be overestimated for other reasons.

When electric power is interrupted to rural homes with wells, the water supply and waste system is interrupted, too. Although the waste system does not require energy input directly, it does require running water. Rural homes most frequently rely on a septic system for waste water. A septic system is a static system relying on gravity for power. The septic system has a dual chamber underground septic tank, which is connected to a drain field. Waste water from the home is carried to a large underground tank with two chambers. Waste water enters the first chamber where a majority of the solids fall to the bottom. They are decomposed over time by anaerobic bacterial action. Liquid is allowed to flow over the top of the first chamber into a second chamber which performs the same function as the first, although the amount of solids is dramatically less. Surface water from the second chamber is allowed to flow to a drain field where the anaerobic bacterial action continues, and the waste water is filtered naturally though the earth as it returns to the water table. A septic system involves periodic removal of the solid wastes from the first chamber, but can last a lifetime and provide a safe solution to liquid wastes for homes beyond the city water and sewer lines. About 15 percent of the homes in America have a well pump and about 25 percent have a septic system. One interesting exception is Indianapolis where much of city still relies on septic tanks.

Thermal Energy

We use thermal energy to keep our homes warm and cool, provide hot water, cook food, and dry our clothes. For air conditioning, electricity is used exclusively. For space heating, water heating, clothes drying, and cooking, a few options normally exist. Common energy sources for space heating are natural gas/propane, heating oil, and electricity, whereas water heating, clothes drying, and cooking typically use either natural gas/propane or electricity. Using electricity for space heating and water heating, the two largest home energy uses, is far less efficient than direct use of natural gas/propane due to the losses associated with generation, transmission, and distribution of electricity. The use of electricity for space and water heating is a misguided practice from the 1950s and 1960s, a poor choice, and very

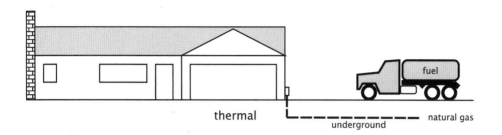

Fuel for home heating is typically supplied by underground natural gas lines in the city and propane or heating fuel trucks in the country.

costly. For our purposes, our space and water heating needs will be supplied by natural gas/propane in all cases. These gaseous fuels have clean products of combustion, carbon dioxide and water. It would make sense wherever practical for homes using electricity for space and water heating to convert to gaseous fuels. It would also make sense for homes using heating oil for space heating and electricity for water heating to convert both to natural gas/propane. For cooking and clothes drying, it is a matter of choice as they represent a small amount of the total home energy needs and have been considered as part of our basic electrical usage.

For urban homes, the preferred source of thermal energy for space heating, water heating, cooking, and clothes drying is natural gas. Natural gas is a clean burning fuel composed primarily of methane that when burned produces carbon dioxide and water. Natural gas is distributed from wells by interstate and intrastate high pressure gas lines, with 40 percent going directly to electric generation and large industrial customers. The other 60 percent is supplied to local distribution companies, some public and some private, who deliver it to each residential and commercial customer in their area or region via special underground gas pipelines. In the United States, there are 257 investor-owned, 931 municipal or publicly-owned, 104 privately-owned, and 15 co-operative local distribution utilities. The investor-owned gas utilities supply gas to 91 percent of residential, commercial, and small industrial customers. A recent trend has been for investor owned electric utilities to merge with gas utilities and call themselves "energy" companies.

Natural gas is a very efficient and clean source of thermal energy for a home. Virtually all the heat energy in the natural gas is used by furnaces and water heaters whose efficiency is typically about 95 percent. If the natural gas was used to generate electricity, more than 70 percent of the heat energy would be lost in generation, transmission, and distribution. For this reason, electric space and water heating is three to four times more expensive and at most one-third as efficient as natural gas. Natural gas is a preferred

fuel for cooking with the combination of direct flame and fast response contributing to its desirability. The clean combustion products -- carbon dioxide and water -- make cooking for family and friends over a gas stove in a closed area for a long period of time safe and commonplace. Natural gas should be the first choice for these things when available.

The gas pipelines normally end at the city limits due to the high cost of serving individual rural customers. Rural homes and businesses have few choices, either propane, heating fuel, or electric. The most popular and useful of these choices is propane or LP gas. In the country beyond the natural gas lines, the most common fuel is propane that is delivered by trucks and stored in a large tank near the home. Propane is a more complex hydrocarbon than natural gas, but the by-products of combustion are the same - carbon dioxide and water. LP gas provides all the versatility of natural gas in that it can be used for space heating, water heating, cooking, and clothes drying with high efficiency. It also has the same safe combustion products. In some cases, home heating fuel delivered by truck to a storage tank is used for home heating in rural areas. Heating oil is only used for space heating and thus the oil heated home would typically use electricity for water heating, cooking, and clothes drying given the unhealthy combustion products of home heating oil. This combination is a poor choice from a cost, efficiency, and environmental standpoint. Converting to propane for the major thermal needs would be beneficial and could be done at a reasonable cost. An oil furnace could be converted to propane or replaced at the end of its useful life. When the electric water heater and clothes dryer reach the end of their useful life, they can be upgraded to propane as well.

As a passing note, both natural gas and propane are excellent fuels for small internal combustion engines, including gensets for producing electricity. Engines converted to operate on these gaseous fuels start easy, have longer life expectancies, and have similarly clean exhaust gases - unlike traditional gasoline or diesel gensets.

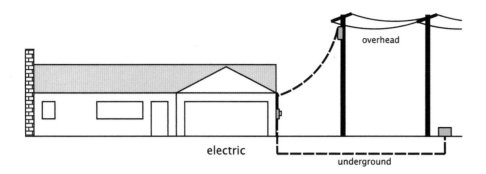

Electricity is always supplied by an electric utility, primarily by overhead lines, to homes in both the city and country. A few newer, more affluent communities are choosing to bury the power lines underground.

Electricity

Let's now examine our electrical usage nationally and individually to understand how much and for what purposes we use electricity.

Our total demand for electricity varies throughout the year in a pattern that is consistent. Usage reaches a peak winter value in December and January due to increased space heating and lighting combined with people spending more time indoors. From a winter peak, demand falls by about 10 percent for a few months until spring before the desire for air conditioning brought on by warmer temperatures leads to a summer peak in July. The summer peak is also the annual peak as demand for air conditioning soars during the hottest days of summer. The summer peak is typically about 20 to 25 percent greater than the winter peak. As autumn arrives, usage falls to a level about equivalent to spring and the cycle repeats.

If we look at daily electrical patterns, a similar situation exists. As we sleep, the need for electricity is at its daily low point. When we awake and set off on our daily routine, electrical demand increases, and continues to increase as businesses open and factories start production. By mid-afternoon, it is at its zenith, and then it slowly subsides as we return home and end our evening by returning to sleep.

We know that all days are not created equal and our usage varies accordingly. The daily demand is fairly consistent during the weekdays, but the change in societal patterns on weekends result in a reduction in demand by about 15 percent.

In the United States, there are over 3,170 electric utilities responsible for ensuring an adequate and reliable source of electricity to all the customers, and there are an additional 2,110 non-utility power producers. The electric utilities are classified by ownership. There are 239 investor-owned, 2,009 publicly-owned or municipals, 912 consumer-owned cooperatives, and 10 federal electric utilities. The 239 investor-owned are by far the largest source of electricity with 75 percent of the nation's generating capacity serving 75 percent of the nation's residential, commercial, and industrial electric customers, although

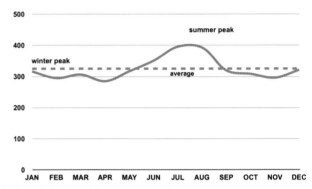

National demand for power varies throughout the year.

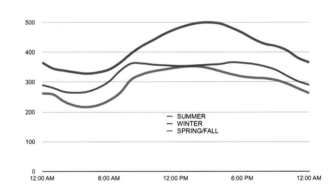

National demand for power varies throughout the day in a common seasonal pattern.

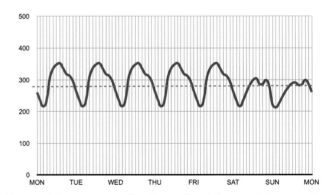

Demand for power varies throughout the week in a predictable pattern within regions of the country.

they represent only 8 percent of the number of electric utilities. The 2,009 publicly-owned electric utilities are nonprofit municipally- or city-owned, many of whom do not have any generating equipment and have a collective generating capacity representing about 10 percent of the national total. The rural cooperatives primarily buy electricity for distribution to rural areas and have 4 percent of the total generating capacity. The federal utilities, primarily dams, account for 10 percent of the nation's generating capacity, but only contribute 1 percent to the retail electric market.

As a nation, electricity is supplied to residential, commercial, and industrial sectors in about equal measures – 37 percent residential, 35 percent commercial, and 28 percent industrial.

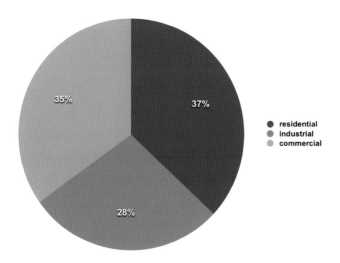

● residential
● industrial
● commercial

Electricity use is divided between residential, commercial, and industrial sectors in nearly equal amounts — 37, 35, and 28 percent.

Energy is a measure of power over a period of time. Electricity is sold on the basis of a unit of energy, which is technically a kilowatt-hour (kWh). If you had ten 100-watt light bulbs, one kilowatt total (10 lights x 100 watt = 1000 watts = 1 kilowatt) operating for one hour, that would be equal to 1 kilowatt-hour, or one unit of energy. On a typical electric bill there will be an accounting of how many units of electrical energy, or kilowatt-hours, were used during the month. The units used are the primary means to determine how much the customer is charged for electricity, plus federal, state, local taxes; service charge; fuel surcharges; and other miscellaneous costs. In 2006, the average cost per unit of energy in the United States was 8.9 cents. It is important to note again that historically electric customers have not been treated equally. Typically industrial users pay the least and residential

users pay the most. In the past, the difference could have been that homes paid as much as 25 times per unit of energy more than industrial users. It still varies widely by region, but on a national basis in 2006, when the average unit price was 8.9 cents, industrial users paid 6.16 cents, commercial users paid 9.46, and residential users paid 10.4 cents.

If we zoom in and examine our detailed annual residential electric usage, we find that in 2001, when a unit of energy was only 8.58 cents, the national average per household was 10,656 units at a cost of $914.28. On a monthly basis that translates into 888 units at $76.19. This converts to an average continuous power of 1,216 watts or 1.216 kilowatts. This is a composite average of all houses that include the full range of electric appliances and equipment. The three largest uses of electricity, which are only used by a percentage of the homes for space heating, water heating, and air conditioning, have a disproportionate effect on these values.

The federal government maintains a list of the most common household appliances which includes some 30-plus items that represent significant uses of electricity in homes. To get a more exact picture of use, let us momentarily remove the energy used for electric space heating in 29 percent of the homes, electric water heating in 38 percent of the homes, and central air conditioning used in 54 percent of homes, just temporarily though, as we will come back to this and consider just those items that are ideally suited for electricity for now. What remains are all the appliances throughout our homes. Virtually every household has a refrigerator, which uses 1,462 units per year, and lights, which account for 940 units per year. After that our independence and individualism comes into play in a major way. For all of the other uses, from significant uses such as clothes washers and dryers (6 percent), freezers (3 percent), televisions (3 percent), and well pumps to a variety of smaller convenience appliances, such as microwaves, computers and everything personal or unique, we lump them into a composite number based on 36 items including the catch all "other."

For these items we use an average of 4,495 units per year. Most people have some or most devices. In the final analysis it all balances out and provides a good representation of how much electricity we typically use. For our purposes we are going to create 3 categories for comparison purposes. Basic electric is lighting, refrigeration, and some of the 36 appliances. All electric is all electric - basic electrical, central air conditioning, space heating, and water heating.

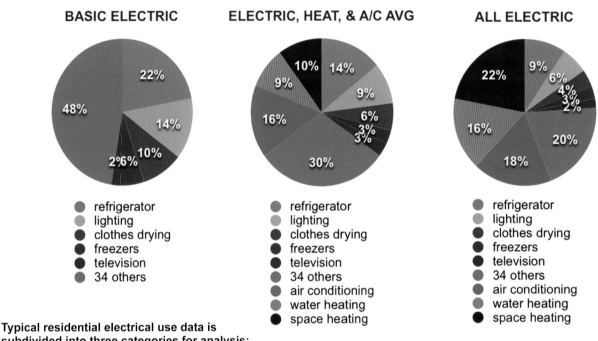

clothes washer	toaster oven	printer	answering machine
clothes dryer	coffee maker	printer/fax/copy	cordless phone
dishwasher	hair dryer	component stereo	pool filter/pump
freezer	television	other stereo	spa heater
furnace fan	VCR/DVD player	dehumidifier	ceiling fan
well pump	cable box	humidifier	waterbed heater
electric range	satellite dish	evaporator/cooler	aquarium heater
electric oven	desktop computer	rechargeable tools	engine block heater
microwave oven	laptop computer	power tools	other(s)

BASIC ELECTRIC

- refrigerator
- lighting
- clothes drying
- freezers
- television
- 34 others

ELECTRIC, HEAT, & A/C AVG

- refrigerator
- lighting
- clothes drying
- freezers
- television
- 34 others
- air conditioning
- water heating
- space heating

ALL ELECTRIC

- refrigerator
- lighting
- clothes drying
- freezers
- television
- 34 others
- air conditioning
- water heating
- space heating

Typical residential electrical use data is subdivided into three categories for analysis: basic electric, composite national average, and all-electric.

Going back to our average home, without electric space and water heating or air conditioning, we use 6,897 units of energy per year, 575 units of energy per month, or 787 watts of power on average. We will categorize this as basic electric for our calculations and round up to 790 watts of continuous power for the average American household for electrical appliances, not including electric space and water heating or air conditioning. The minimum value on the low end for all homes is for the refrigerator and lights, which account for an annual usage of 2,402 kilowatt hours, or about 275 watts continuous.

In the United States, space heating accounts for 10 percent of all electricity used; water heating accounts for 9 percent; and central air conditioning accounts for 16 percent. Electricity is used for space heating in 29 percent of homes and adds an average of 3,524 kilowatt hours annually to those households for an average of 400 watts. Electric water heating is used in 38 percent of homes and adds an average of 2,552 kilowatt hours annually for each household, which amounts to an average of 290 watts. Electricity is used exclusively for air conditioning in 54 percent of homes and adds an average 2,796 kilowatt hours annually for an average of 320 watts continuous.

On a national basis, for an all-electric home we can add the basic electric usage of 790 watts, space heating of 400 watts, water heating of 290 watts, and air conditioning of 320 watts for a total average of 1,800 watts or 15,768 kilowatt hours annually, more

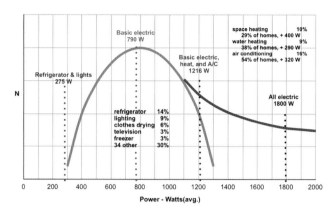

The relative number of homes compared to the amount of power usage by category

than doubling (227 percent) the household electrical energy use. It should be noted that the all-electric home chart is representative of how we generally use energy in our homes. Home heating and air conditioning, plus water heating, use 56 percent on average and everything else uses 44 percent.

A summary chart of our electrical usage identifies four key points: a minimum usage of 275 watts for a refrigerator and lights; 790 watts for basic electrical usage; an overall average of 1,216 watts, including space/water heating and air conditioning in a portion of the homes; and 1,800 watts for an all-electric home.

Characteristics of our Electric Supply System

Prior to the Civil War, there were more than 20 different railroad track widths, between three and six feet, in use in the United States, and it was not possible for any train to run on a track of a different width. Congress established the width for the transcontinental railway at 4 feet, 8.5 inches, a popular width, and that is what they all measure today. Every technology establishes common rules or standards on the pathway to commercialization. Electricity is no different and from varied beginnings in the early years of experimentation, three popular supply systems would become prominent in most homes in the United States over the years.

• Thomas Edison's 110 volt direct current for early urban systems

• Nikola Tesla and George Westinghouse's 120-volt alternating current, 60 hertz, which is today's standard

• Charles Kettering's 32-volt direct current for farm electric systems

It is not altogether clear how 110 volts and 120 volts were established. I have heard a few explanations and lean toward one that begins with Edison at about the time he was developing his central station system. Contrary to the desires of his financiers to sell electrical equipment into the market for consumers, Edison wanted to control it all and sell electricity from his power plants through wires. The first plant was the Vulcan Street Power Station, an 800-watt hydropower plant in Appleton, Wisconsin, which was followed closely by the coal and steam powered Pearl Street Station in New York's financial district. Both of them used 110 volts and were direct current. The size of a power plant in 1882 was limited by the size of the steam engines or rivers and dams that could drive the generators to produce the electricity. There were also technical difficulties and safety implications with higher direct current voltages. The Edison business model anticipated that one large coal steam engine plant could serve an area within one mile. This combined with technical influences and other economic factors, such as the cost and size of wires, and the cost of equipment, led him to establish his system voltage at 110. Remember that direct current can not be easily changed from one voltage to another.

Tesla and Westinghouse developed their alternating current system a little later and had a distinct advantage for selling electricity that would beat Edison at his own game, at least temporarily. The single greatest advantage of alternating current is that the voltage can easily be changed. With the alternating current system, electricity could be generated at a higher voltage, increased to the highest voltage for transmission over long distances, reduced to an intermediate voltage for distribution within a town or city, and finally reduced to a user voltage of 120. I suspect they were adapting to the existing equipment as light bulbs and other early equipment could operate equally on alternating or direct current. Although it can get confusing when you look at nameplate ratings on appliances and see 110, 112, 115, 120, 208, 220, 230, and 240, the most common electrical characteristics supplied at the electric meter to your home and business today is 120/240 volts alternating current, single-phase. All but the very largest of appliances operate at 120 volts alternating current, and that's what is in all of our homes. Furnaces, ranges, air conditioners, and electric dryers may typically use the higher voltage.

With Kettering and the Delco-Light plant it was different in that the electricity was generated within several feet of where it was used and thus did not have to be transmitted at all. Secondly, Kettering started long after the bitter debate between Edison and Westinghouse over the safety of alternating current had simmered down and had the benefit of better information regarding electrical safety. During the engineering phase from 1913 to 1915, 32 volts was chosen purely for safety against shock hazards. Early product literature proudly states the "Delco-Light 32 volt service is safe. There is no danger of serious or fatal shocks. Tests have shown that it requires 40 volts to break through the skin tissue." He was ahead of his time and very attuned with the state of understanding. History would prove him absolutely right on this point.

Science, experience, and critical analysis have taught us that the human body has two elements that resist the flow of electricity through our bodies, our skin and all of our internal muscles and organs. Our skin has a fairly high resistance, but it is very thin and can easily be broken by an arc prior to touching a high voltage, so for safety matters it is normally neglected. Our internal resistance is very low and reflects our composition from our salt water origins of life. Simply put, we are great conductors of electricity, 500 ohms is the value used.

In establishing safe voltage levels, standards organizations consider both the person and conditions of use. The general public includes all persons from toddlers to seniors. Infants, patients in hospitals, and other vulnerable persons have special requirements in our electrical standards. A primary condition of use that is always evaluated is the proximity or potential exposure to water. In homes, the living room, dining room, and bedroom are considered "dry" locations. Bathrooms, kitchens, laundry rooms, garages, and outdoor areas are classified as "damp" or "wet." The generally agreed upon threshold voltages, the voltage below which potentially fatal conditions do not exist, for alternating current and direct current are as follows.

- Dry conditions
  - 60 volts direct current
  - 30 volts alternating current

- Damp or wet conditions
  - 30 volts direct current
  - 15 volts alternating current

Over the years, accidental death by electrocution increased steadily for nearly 75 years with the popularity and spread of electricity. Improvements in our electrical codes and standards have reversed this trend in homes in recent years to a level of 400 to 500 deaths per year in the United States. This has been the result primarily of better grounding methods and "supplementary measures," such as ground fault circuit interrupter (GFCI) protection.

Another aspect of Kettering's approach to providing the convenience of electricity under absolutely safe conditions was that his farm electric plant was "isolated," and not a "grounded" system. An isolated system has the advantage of "inherent" double fault protection. This method requires that two faults or failures occur in the basic protective system before a hazardous condition exists.

Regarding the electrical characteristics of a future system, a few science matters should be considered and stated.

- Alternating current voltage can be easily changed with a transformer.

- Direct current voltage cannot be easily changed.

- Changing direct current to alternating current is complicated, inefficient, and expensive.

- Changing alternating current to direct current is simple, efficient, and inexpensive.

The primary benefit of alternating current is for large power plants to generate electricity to transmit over long distances and distribute regionally. It provides no benefit to the consumer of electricity in homes and most businesses that could not be provided by direct current electricity at a safe voltage. As a result, every electrical device or appliance in our homes and businesses has been sold to us for the convenience of the alternating current network. Ironically, many modern devices convert 120-volt alternating current to a lower direct current voltage for their use, such as computers, printers, cell phones, cordless drills, shavers, and any device with a "plastic brick" in the power cord. It would not be very complicated for the electric utilities to supply a safe direct current voltage to homes and businesses.

To facilitate commercial solar and wind technology, and to make our homes electrically safer, I believe that a standard direct current voltage for all homes in the future should be established at 48 volts exclusively. I chose this because it is below the safe level of 60 volts in dry conditions, has several ancillary technical benefits over lower voltages and most certainly higher voltages. Supplementary protective measures can be provided for safe use in wet conditions as we do now for 120-volt alternating current in our homes. I am, however, open to considering lower voltages. I feel it is more important to select a standard to move forward than to endlessly debate the need to transition to a low-voltage direct current system in our homes. Given a choice, I would never select alternating current or 120 volts for use in our homes, and I will use 48-volts direct current as we go forward.

The national transition to safe direct current electricity in our homes would be large and lengthy, but could be accomplished without much disruption in the normal replacement cycle of electric equipment. The most important secondary aspect of doing this is for the benefit of solar and wind technologies to enable people and businesses to own their own electric power plants. Renewable technologies require storage to bring a varying supply and demand together successfully. Solar and wind technologies must have appliances and equipment that operate directly from them or through batteries, just as Kettering had envisioned when he developed his system.

This is a perfect transition for the most important point of this book, that rather than buying electricity, we take a giant step forward into the past where individuals and businesses invested in privately-owned independent electric generating equipment.

From the analysis of our electricity usage, we found that the average power required for basic electric needs in a home was 790 watts. For an all-electric home, the average power value increased to 1,800 watts.

As a point of reference, the portable generator providing power to the camper's computer is from a current product brochure. It is rated 1,000 watts and is the smallest generator they make. It weighs 29 pounds and measures 18 inches-by-10 inches-by-15 inches in size. The second smallest generator they make is rated 2,000 watts. It weighs 47 pounds and is a little larger in size - 20 inches-by-12 inches-by-17 inches. Technically speaking, if these units were connected to a suitable battery set to accommodate variations in demand and periods of high demand, they would be able to supply the basic electrical needs of the average home and the average all-electric home, respectively, with a little extra capacity to spare.

The downside is that the genset would consume gasoline, run continuously, and have to be rebuilt after several thousand hours. It is also fair to acknowledge that the efficiency of the genset would be about 25 percent or roughly equivalent to the central station steam generating plant and transmission and distribution system. I wonder what would happen if we applied the hybrid concept from the farm electric plant to accomplish the same results. What would be the effect of a larger genset or solar panels or possibly a wind generator? I know from my experience that solar panels with an area that is one quarter to one third of the square footage of the average home could easily supply all of the basic electrical and air conditioning needs to that home. Some very sunny places will require an even smaller area or may have enough excess power for new uses. I also know from experience that a modern wind generator of a reasonable size can do the same in many regions of the country where the wind is reasonably strong. Let's examine how this can be done, the potential in both rural and urban areas, and the national impact of doing so.

A camper uses a portable generator for generating electricity.
Source: www.hondapowerequipment.com.

Chapter 9

RURAL RE-ELECTRIFICATION

I must confess that I backed into my understanding of the farm electric plant through an interest in the wind-driven generators during my senior year in engineering school in 1972. When I found out that wind-driven generators were actually manufactured in the 1930s and 1940s and that some could still be found in the Great Plains, I borrowed a pick-up truck and did the obvious - I drove to the Great Plains to find and buy some. At the time, when I would buy a Jacobs or Wincharger, the farmer would usually ask if I was interested in the Delco-Light or any of the 32-volt direct current appliances. I thought for a moment and said yes, and so I wound up buying a couple Delco-Light plants and some 32-volt motors and appliances. It would be awhile until I came to appreciate the significance and magnitude of all the companies and all the equipment produced for farm electric plants.

Something that I came to understand was how important Charles Kettering's Delco- Light farm electric plant really was in establishing the fundamental system design parameters and creating a market for these products. Like the electric system he developed for the automobile five years earlier, the Delco-Light plant was an incredibly insightful and elegant design that has enduring significance today. Before we look forward to a modern hybrid electric plant, the Delco-Light plant can serve as the basis for establishing the system configuration and hardware details for meeting the range of modern needs.

A second thing that Kettering did was to develop a "family" of rural electric plants. During the 31 years in production, more than 100 models were offered, but they could all be reduced to five basic models. The three smaller models were rated 500, 750, and 1,000 watts and used a 32-volt battery. The two larger models, rated 1,250 to 1,500 watts and 2,500 to 3,000 watts, were available for use with both 32-volt and 112-volt batteries. The 32-volt models were by far the most popular and the 112-volt models were generally used for larger power needs and bigger buildings. A close reading of the original Delco product literature offers the potential uses for each model, as follows:

• Delco-Light 500 watt - "summer cottages, small farms, camps, and motor boats (actually small yachts in modern parlance)"

• Delco-Light 750 watt, the most popular model - "farms, country homes, schools, churches, and hotels"

• Delco-Light 1,000 watt - "general farm service and motion picture theaters" in small towns (the iconic small town theatre and "talkies" were the rage at the time)

• Delco-Light 1,250 to 3,000 watt - "large farms, hotels, country clubs, and estates"

A final important thing that Kettering did, which has remained a cornerstone of his success and genius, was to offer a complete selection of utilization equipment for his electric plants. This included Delco deep and shallow well pumps, as well as all of the favorite appliances of the day that were popular in the city, including clothes washers, vacuum cleaners, refrigerators, coffee percolators, irons, clippers, toasters, and even a mechanical power stand to operate belt-driven farm equipment. All of this equipment operated on direct current at 32 volts. The availability of a complete range of electrical appliances capable of operating on direct current over the normal range of battery voltage was fundamental to his success. It is also a fundamental element to a modern grid-free hybrid power plant using solar and wind power.

The most forward-looking feature was the openness of the system architecture to other electric sources, specifically wind generators and solar photovoltaic panels. In the 1930s, long after the introduction of the Delco-Light plant, 32-volt wind generators were introduced to the market and could be used as stand-alone power plants or simply added to a farm electric plant to make it a wind-genset-battery hybrid. The effect for Delco-Light owners was reduced fuel use and genset running time, which increased engine life expectancy proportionally. If you had a Delco-Light plant today, the same effect could be achieved by adding a few solar panels to create a solar-genset-battery hybrid. Add a wind generator and you would have a wind-solar-genset-battery hybrid. Thus the engine would operate even less frequently, namely just during long periods of clouds with little wind or very high short-term power needs, and last even longer. If we start to design a new hybrid power plant for the needs of today and the future, the system architecture, range of power capability, and availability of utilization equipment pioneered by Kettering in his Delco-Light plant remain a fundamental part of the design and engineering process. The technological advances that have occurred since Kettering designed the Delco-Light plant have been significant and contribute a great deal to the practicality and reliability of a modern hybrid power plant.

In recent times, there have been a number of noteworthy advances. The size and weight of the engine generators have become increasingly smaller. A 1,000-watt Delco-Light genset weighed 360 pounds and measured 20-by-25-by-32 inches. A modern equivalent genset weighs 29 pounds and measures 18-by-10-by-15 inches. Material technology advances offer unlimited capability to affect each of the products associated, not only with the power plant but for the utilization equipment. Photovoltaic panels are commonly available from a variety of high quality manufacturers and more are sure to come. The digital information age offers unimagined smart control, using weather data, usage patterns, and other control inputs to optimize system performance. New fuels and promising biofuels have become available, or will be in the future.

The starting point of this exercise is the median U.S. home in 2001 for a very specific purpose. Over the years, the question is frequently asked "Can 'it' provide ALL my power?" Detractors to solar and wind energy have frequently implied solar and wind energy means a lowering of our standard of living, "freezing in the dark in caves." The answer to the first question is unequivocally "yes," which addresses the second point of view. A few points should also be considered. The first is that a case can be made that individually we use just about as much electricity as we will reasonably need now and will not increase our demand in the foreseeable future. With all the work, needs, and wants for which we rely on electricity, I would say we have it pretty good. The second is that a case can also be made that we can easily fulfill our needs with electricity more efficiently and less wastefully, with no "lowering of our standard of living" or measurable effect on our ways.

In this exercise we are going to specify a family of hybrid electric power plants - small, medium, and large. Thus we will use a medium hybrid for the median house, a smaller hybrid with half the rating for lower power needs, and a large hybrid with twice the rating for larger power needs. I would point out that the median home could migrate to the smaller power system through efficiency, thoughtful use, and best practices to reduce the "average" power use without any sacrifice in convenience, which will go a long way towards the affordability of owning your own electric plant. I would also point out that this same downward migration in average power use through efficiency and conservation will have the same effect on larger power users. The net effect is to include more potential users and expand the market significantly. It is your decision as to whether to do it and how to go about accomplishing it.

A hybrid power system is a "hybrid," because it combines two or more devices to take advantage of the benefits of each to counter the disadvantages of the other with the result being an overall improvement in performance. In our case, we are combining a battery with a genset, solar panels, and a wind generator as sources, alone or in any combination, into a system to produce electricity. In all cases, the battery is a central component and is always included. The engine provides the benefit of electricity on demand and is normally included in all systems but is not mandatory. The wind generator or the solar electric can be added separately, together, or not at all. The system is modular enough to start with a basic system and add other sources at any point in the future, or perhaps sources that have yet to be invented. The system design is also open enough to accept components from each of the three systems to cross over to another system, and to adjust battery sizes to optimize the capability and results.

The process begins by first summarizing our goals and objectives to develop the requirements for our medium hybrid power plant. The power plant must reliably produce a continuous supply of electricity to operate the basic electrical needs (790 watts continuous average), plus a central air conditioning system (320 watts continuous average), for a median home with 2,000 square feet of living space. The power plant will include a battery to compensate for variations in supply and demand and provide for high-peak demand in the home. The overall system will use propane as the thermal fuel for the genset, if included, and space and water heating. Collectively, these components will provide for all the common home utility needs, including the water and septic system, basic electric power, central air conditioning, and fuel for space and water heating.

Our medium hybrid electric system for the median home will be rated at 4,800 watts. The rating for the smaller and larger models will be 2,400 watts and 9,600 watts, respectively. These ratings are based on using the nominal battery voltage rating of 48 combined with current ratings of 50, 100, and 200 amps. The average continuous power rating of the small, medium, and large hybrid will be 400 watts, 800 watts, and 1,600 watts, respectively. The range of continuous power for the family of hybrid electric plants is from 300 to 2,000 watts, or in other words enough to supply every home on our national usage chart from a refrigerator and lights to the all-electric home, which covers the vast majority of homes in

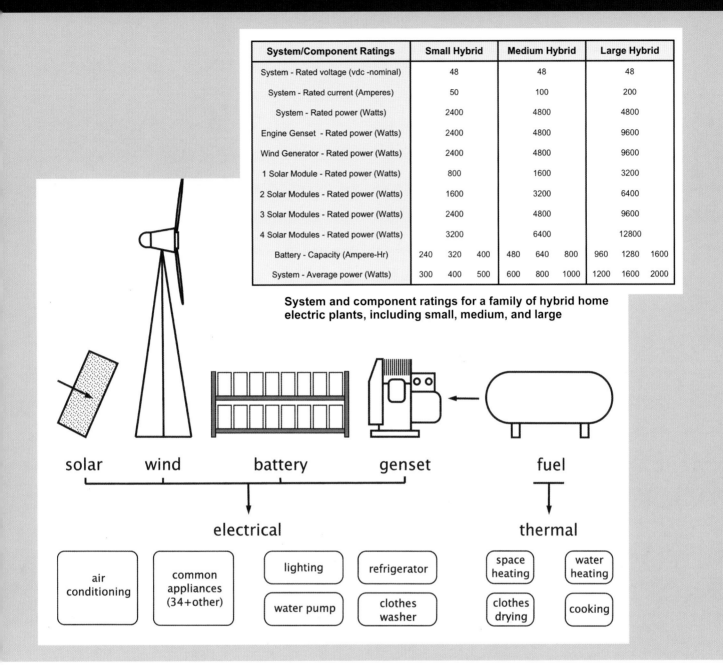

System/Component Ratings	Small Hybrid			Medium Hybrid			Large Hybrid		
System - Rated voltage (vdc -nominal)	48			48			48		
System - Rated current (Amperes)	50			100			200		
System - Rated power (Watts)	2400			4800			4800		
Engine Genset - Rated power (Watts)	2400			4800			9600		
Wind Generator - Rated power (Watts)	2400			4800			9600		
1 Solar Module - Rated power (Watts)	800			1600			3200		
2 Solar Modules - Rated power (Watts)	1600			3200			6400		
3 Solar Modules - Rated power (Watts)	2400			4800			9600		
4 Solar Modules - Rated power (Watts)	3200			6400			12800		
Battery - Capacity (Ampere-Hr)	240	320	400	480	640	800	960	1280	1600
System - Average power (Watts)	300	400	500	600	800	1000	1200	1600	2000

System and component ratings for a family of hybrid home electric plants, including small, medium, and large

solar   wind   battery   genset   fuel

electrical   thermal

air conditioning	common appliances (34+other)	lighting	refrigerator
		water pump	clothes washer

space heating	water heating
clothes drying	cooking

the United States. This range of power capability is also compatible with the electric needs of many businesses. From these system ratings, we will determine the specifics of each of the component parts, including battery, engine, solar, and finally wind, which is the most complicated.

The battery is the central component and its advantages include energy storage, silent operation, very high short-term power capability, reliability, and overall system stability. It operates at a high efficiency and is a very simple static device with a long life and high residual value. Another positive attribute is that the lead-acid battery is the most highly recycled product in the world at 98 percent. The standard lead-acid deep cycle battery design, Exide ironclad, used with the original Delco-Light plants would be perfectly suitable and acceptable for use in a modern system, if it was still in production. Although there have been minor advancements in technology and manufacturing, excellent batteries are commercially available and ready for use in our hybrid electric plant today. In fact, several battery manufacturers are capable of providing high quality battery cells in the range of sizes required for our hybrid systems. A lead-acid battery is essentially heavy by nature which is acceptable since it remains stationary for its useful life. Weight is not a concern for a stationary battery because it is only moved twice, once when delivered and once when it is exchanged for recycling decades later.

The individual lead-acid cells of the appropriate size are normally connected together to form a

Original Exide Ironclad battery had the characteristics and performance to meet modern requirements.

battery. Since the nominal voltage rating of each lead-acid cell is 2 volts, a 48-volt system would consist of 24 individual cells. The cells are interconnected and set on suitable storage racks where they remain for their entire service life. The size of a battery is specified in terms of "capacity," or ampere-hours, and is determined by the general size of the system. For our medium hybrid, an ideal battery capacity would be 640 ampere-hours at the eight-hour rate. This essentially means that the battery will deliver a total of 640 amps during an eight-hour period at a rate of 80 amps. It is a rating system that is based on standard controlled conditions and used for comparative purposes between battery models. In practice, a battery in our system would receive and supply current from relatively small to medium levels. The demand would be well within the capability of the battery to deliver and a small percentage of the maximum capability of the battery. Over a short period, the battery could deliver several hundred amps and thus meet any demand placed upon it.

So for our medium hybrid, the battery will have a rated capacity of 640 ampere-hours and thus be capable of storing 30.7 kilowatt hours or units of electricity. The battery for the smaller and larger systems will be half and twice the capacity, 320 ampere-hours and 1,280 ampere-hours, respectively. Why 640 ampere hours for the battery size? The first reason is I used to have a friend who was a battery scientist at a major manufacturer. He was the type of person who exuded knowledge and confidence when you spoke to him. When I asked him at what is the best rate to charge a battery, he said the eight-hour rate. If our system and genset rating is 4,800 watts and our continuous use is 790 watts, then the amount of power going into the battery from the genset when it is operating is a little over 4,000 watts, or 80 amps at 48 volts. The 80 amps times eight hours gives us the 640 ampere-hours rating and the same process is true for rating of the small and large systems. Secondly, if we do a similar exercise with a Delco-Light plant, the result would be close. The most popular

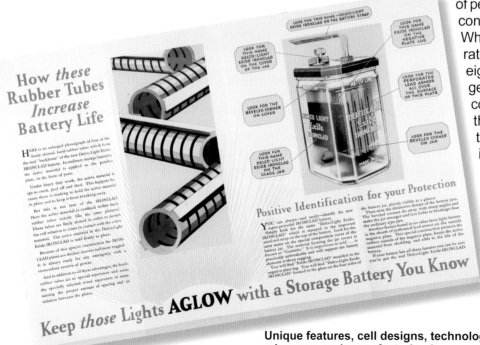

Unique features, cell designs, technology advances, and manufacturing improvements make the lead-acid battery even better for use today.

unit sold was rated 750 watts, and the standard battery was rated 160 ampere hours. If we assume, as we have above, that about one-sixth of the power is going directly to operate equipment and the balance of about 20 amps is going into the battery, then the ideal battery size would be 160 ampere hours. I think this a good rule of thumb to use to determine battery capacity.

Furthermore, it is reasonable to allow the battery capacity for each of these systems to vary by as much as 25 percent, up or down, for higher or lower usage levels than the rated power values of 400, 800, and 1,600 watts. Implicit in this is the ability to bridge the gap between the average power performance of the systems and to extend the lower and upper limits - the small hybrid with a larger battery approaches the medium hybrid with a smaller battery, a medium hybrid with a larger battery approaches a large hybrid with a smaller battery, and the small hybrid with a small battery and large hybrid with a larger battery extend the capabilities. The net effect is a power capability that spans the range of residential electric use from the most basic refrigerator and lights to a very large and sophisticated modern family home. The capability of these three hybrid systems can be optimized over the entire range of continuous average power needs from 300 watts to 2,000 watts. Given the modularity of the system design, we can also address needs less than 300 watts with a simple solar battery hybrid in many regions.

I mentioned that the battery provides stability to the system, and it does in that it resists large changes in voltages between high states of charge and discharge. Additionally, the battery voltage, at rest, is reasonably representative of the state of charge and thus whether a battery is fully charged, partially charged, or nearly discharged. When we speak of a 2-volt nominal cell, we recognize that it is normal for this voltage to vary with the state of charge and the rate at which it is receiving or delivering electricity, or amps. The terminal voltage of a static lead-acid battery cell that is fully charged would be 2.2 volts. If we discharged it at the eight-hour rate and allowed it to stabilize for a short while, the battery terminal voltage would be 1.75 volts per cell. If we charged it to a little over half-full, or until the terminal voltage was 2, and the genset began to charge it, the cell voltages would rise a predictable amount based on the rate of charging. If we stopped charging and began discharging the cell, the voltage would fall a predictable amount based on the rate of discharge. The values can vary with different size batteries, but for a given battery the system voltage is a useful and

effective control value. As we will see, the advances in data acquisition and control since the early days offer great opportunities to improve system performance in a dramatic way.

A battery performs best at a normal indoor temperature of 75 degrees Fahrenheit. When a battery approaches full state-of-charge, it is common for the water in the solution to electrolyze and give off small amounts hydrogen gas. Over a long period, the "gassing" may require that distilled water be added periodically to replace the water lost and maintain the correct electrolyte chemistry. From a practical standpoint, thermal, ventilation, and watering access can be provided with a simple enclosure in most cases. Additional methods for dealing with temperature extremes are readily available.

Although the battery is a remarkable device with many good attributes, it does not create electricity. An engine connected to a generator can create electricity from fuel, as long as it has fuel. The primary source in the Delco-Light plant was the engine-generator set, or genset, and its power rating determined the system rating. The genset for our medium hybrid system will be rated at 4,800 watts, the small 2,400 watts, and the large 9,600 watts. You might ask, why have a generator that is six times larger than the power needed? Basically, the answer is so that we don't hear it running five-sixths of the time and it will last for six times as many years. With thoughtful and efficient use practices and a little wind and/or solar electricity, it is conceivable to reduce the genset operation to 5 percent of the time or less, and thus extend its life expectancy to several decades. The characteristics that preclude a genset from simply being used all the time are the cost of fuel, noise, exhaust gases, heat, and life expectancy. The advantages of the battery, wind, and solar sources are thus used to offset these disadvantages in a hybrid power plant.

In Kettering's day, the fuel choices were limited to gasoline and kerosene. Although gasoline units were sold originally, gasoline was a concern for storage and the preferred fuel became kerosene. Kerosene was used in lamps, as home heating fuel, and as a "cheap" alternative for early tractors. It has safer vaporization characteristics for storage. As a point of reference, coal was the primary fuel for heating in the cities. Since that time, gaseous fuels, such as natural gas and propane, have become the ubiquitous and preferred fuel sources for heating.

In the city, homes and businesses receive gas from underground pipelines operated by local gas distribution utilities which are connected to major underground lines that are in turn connected to huge underground natural gas wells. Natural gas is an excellent fuel for space heating, water heating, clothes drying, and cooking, which collectively can account for as much as two-thirds of a home's energy needs. They are highly efficient in giving up heat energy, typically in the mid-90 percent range, and are very clean burning. The products of combustion are carbon dioxide and water.

Since the underground gas lines are prohibitively expensive to install in rural and remote areas, natural gas is not an option but could be. Kerosene and home heating fuel are still used in some areas of the country, but the preferred fuel for space and water heating is propane, sometimes called "bottled gas" or LPG, which is widely available in remote and rural areas. A ride in the country will reveal large white and silver propane tanks in a variety of sizes on homes, farms, and cabins everywhere. Propane is very similar to natural gas in that it is equally clean burning and highly efficient for space heating, water heating, clothes drying, and cooking. It will be our fuel of choice for our hybrid thermal electric plant. We will use propane for space and water heating and as the fuel for our genset.

Engines operating on gaseous fuels, propane and natural gas, in addition to producing clean exhaust gases, will start easier, require less maintenance, and have a longer life expectancy than equivalent gasoline models. Most small gasoline engines can be easily adapted to operate on gaseous fuels and most of the manufacturers of popular small engines offer gaseous fuel options or conversion kits. Engines that are within these power ranges are air-cooled, spark-ignition, and similar in size to a single cylinder lawn mower engine for our small hybrid and a two cylinder riding lawn mower engine for our medium hybrid. For the large hybrid, a small liquid-cooled engine may be considered as well as a compression-ignition or diesel engine. A benefit of a liquid-cooled engine is that the waste heat can be captured and used. Another benefit of a diesel engine is compatibility with farms using diesel equipment and perhaps transitioning to local bio-diesel in the future.

One advantage of starting with a clean sheet of paper is that the components can be idealized. This is especially important for the engine. In typical use, a small engine operates at different speeds and a wide range of conditions at any given speed. At all of these conditions, there is a fuel efficiency associated with it, and at one speed and one condition the fuel efficiency is better than at any other point. Interestingly, operating at that one point is also beneficial to

an engine's life expectancy, which is a plus. Normally, small portable alternating current gensets operate at either 3,600 or 1,800 rpm to yield a frequency of 60 hertz. At 3,600 rpm, the engine is small, noisy, doesn't last very long, and is not all that efficient when operating over varying conditions. At 1,800 rpm, the engine is twice as large, half as noisy, lasts twice as long, costs twice as much and is not all that efficient when operating over varying conditions either. For our direct current genset, the battery allows the engine to operate at its most efficient point at all times. In conjunction with the fuel benefits, the idealized speed will improve life expectancy and have reasonable noise characteristics. A normal speed range to achieve this best fuel economy would most likely fall in the range of 2,400 to 2,600 rpm.

Operating an engine at the optimum point allows us to design a direct current generator that is matched to the engine for this specific condition. A few successful manufacturers of farm electric plant equipment during the 1930s and 1940s still manufacture a very suitable line of single and twin cylinder engines in the 7 to 24 horsepower range that would be perfectly suited to our hybrid power plant. In fact, one of these manufacturers sells a genset to the telecommunications industry that has a 48-volt output at a maximum power rating of 6,000 watts. Since it's close to what we need, we will rate it 4,800 watts for the best fuel efficiency point and use it for our medium hybrid. For the small hybrid, there are several single-cylinder engines in the 8 to 11 horsepower range available that would be suitable and are capable of operating on gaseous fuels. In fact, the most popular RV, marine, and vehicle generators would be excellent configurations and could be easily converted and optimized for home hybrid service for the small and medium systems. An outdoor enclosure is especially desirable for reducing the genset noise and providing an added measure of environmental protection for the components.

At this point, our median home has a two-cylinder, air-cooled, propane genset rated 4,800 watts in an outdoor enclosure next to a large LPG tank. The propane supplies all of the thermal energy directly for space and water heating. The genset, which operates about 15 to 20 percent of the time, converts the propane to electricity for direct use or storage in the lead-acid batteries. Together they provide 100 percent of the basic electricity to our country home for refrigeration, lights, water pumping, and a combination of 36 other common appliances. If we want to add central air conditioning, it means the genset will run 5 to 20 percent more frequently during the

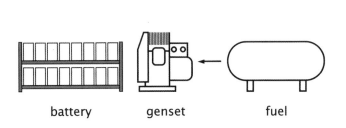

The most basic hybrid includes a genset and battery identical to the Delco-Light plant.

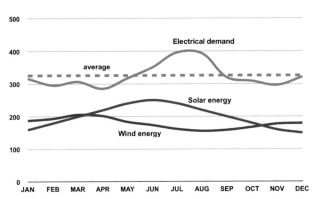

Comparison of annual electrical demand and the availability of solar and wind energy

summer months, depending on the average local temperature.

The propane cost for our home remains the same for space and water heating. However, producing electricity with the genset consumes additional fuel and that costs money. If we want to include air conditioning it will consume even more fuel. Although the genset run-time is reduced by the battery to 15 to 20 percent year-round and increased 5 to 20 percent more in the summer for air conditioning, the fuel use and shorter genset life are issues. The solution is to look to solar and wind energy to reduce fuel use, extend genset life, and improve overall system performance.

Converting the light energy from the sun and kinetic energy in the wind into electricity for our hybrid can deliver huge benefits. It is important to understand how these two variable energy sources behave individually as well as how they interact on a short- and long-term basis.

The sun is overhead half of each day beginning with sunrise and ending with sunset, whereas the wind can blow at anytime during the day. In the northern hemisphere, the sun has a more direct path and thus provides more energy in summer than in winter when the tilt of the earth's axis reduces the angle of the sun's rays to minimize the atmosphere's filtering effect.

The average wind speed is typically higher in the winter than in the summer, which is the opposite of the sun. In many areas, seasonal cloud cover and shorter days act to further reduce solar energy in the winter. In contrast, frequently high-energy winds are associated with weather and storm-related activities, which also include increased cloud cover. What evolves is a symbiotic relationship between the wind and sun on both a short- and long-term basis that provides a more consistent supply of energy overall.

Geographically, on a wind energy map of the United States, we find adequate wind energy in vast regions of the country, but primarily in the upper Midwest. On the solar energy map, the southern-tier states where the winds are not strong is where solar energy is in abundance. In virtually all areas both are available to some degree, and in some areas they are both available in adequate or abundant amounts, which is the best situation. The other relationship to note is that in the northern states the wind is more abundant in the winter months and coincides with the peak winter demand for power. Correspondingly, solar energy is at its peak during the summer months in the southern states when electricity demand is greatest for air conditioning. To make matters better, the peak usage of electricity for air conditioning between one o'clock and three o'clock in the afternoon coincides with the peak production time of solar panels. This is a very good situation. Comparing annual electricity demand with the availability of solar energy, we see a good correlation between solar energy and peak summer demand from air conditioning.

Since photovoltaic panels are readily commercially available and can easily be added in power increments, we will start with solar electricity first. A solar panel is an amazing device, and had it been discovered 100 years earlier, our electric world would be dramatically different. From an important discovery at Bell Laboratories in 1954, the commercially viable solar cell technology has moved steadily forward and is contributing more each year to meet our needs from the smallest uses to larger electric-generating arrays. A solar panel is a grouping of photovoltaic cells that simply converts the sun's light energy into electricity.

A common solar panel is about 5-feet high by 3-feet wide, and a few inches thick with glazing, and is rated about 200-watts peak at 12-volts direct current. For the medium hybrid, eight of the panels are connected together to form a "solar module" with an output of 48 volts. It would have a maximum power rating of 1,600 watts and be 12-feet wide by 10-feet high. A single module could be connected into our hybrid and effect a reduction in fuel use and genset

Wind energy potential in the United States. Source: National Renewable Energy Laboratory, Golden, Colorado.

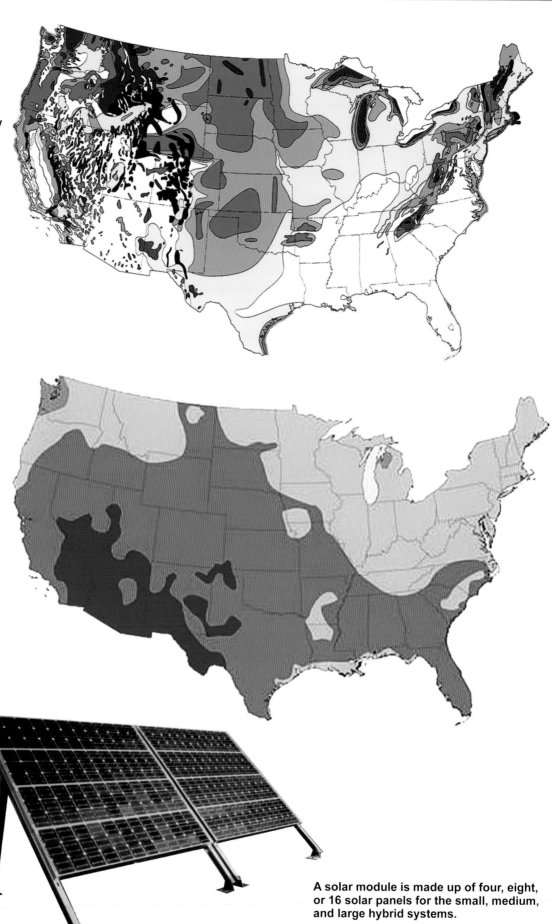

Solar energy potential in the United States

A solar module is made up of four, eight, or 16 solar panels for the small, medium, and large hybrid systems.

operating time. Up to three additional modules can be added until the combined power rating is 33 percent greater than our system rating. In other words, depending on the number of modules – from one to four – our medium hybrid could have 1,600, 3,200, 4,800, or 6,400 watts of solar electricity. All four modules would be 12 feet by 40 feet long and could easily fit on 500 square feet of the roof of a 2,000-square-foot home. For the small hybrid, four panels will be connected together as a solar module and would have a maximum power-rating of 800 watts. Similarly, the large hybrid would have 16 panels per solar module and a power-rating of 3,200 watts. The ability to add up to three additional modules is thus extended to the small and large hybrids, as well.

On a clear day, each solar panel would start to produce electricity shortly after sunrise and increase to a peak around noon, before tapering off before sunset. As we can see from the graph, a point on the line represents the power (watts) at any given time and the area beneath the line represents the energy (watt-hours) produced by the panel during the day. If we divide the energy by the number of hours in the whole day, we get the average power (watts).

With the changes in the sun's angles during the year, the seasonal variation in hours of daylight, and constantly changing, but statistically predictable, weather patterns, estimating the power produced at a given location can make you dizzy. One method that I have preferred for a long time is establishing an average continuous power value for estimating power from a solar panel. In theory, it goes like this: If I mount a solar panel in a south-facing fixed position and measure the energy produced for one year and divide it by the hours in a year, I will have an average continuous power value. For example, a 100-watt solar panel facing south at an angle of 39 degrees in Salina, Kansas in one year might produce 175,520 watt-hours of energy, which is a pretty reasonable value for Salina, in my opinion. Dividing that by the number of hours in a year, the result would be a final average continuous power value of 20 watts, which takes into consideration all the sun's angles, nighttime hours, and weather patterns. For general calculations, I simply multiply the solar panel maximum power rating by 0.20, or 20 percent, to estimate average continuous power and energy. It should be obvious that a solar panel would probably produce 30 percent more in Tucson, Arizona and 30 percent less in the Pacific Northwest. The values for the multiplier would thus be 0.25 in Tucson and 0.15 in Portland. On the other hand, Tucson probably needs more electricity for air conditioning than Salina, and Portland

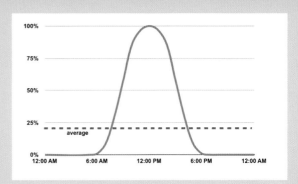

Daily solar panel output

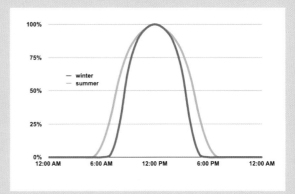

Daily solar panel output varies seasonally.

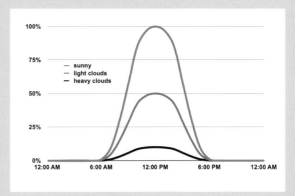

Daily solar panel output varies with cloud cover.

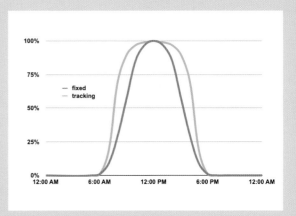

Daily solar panel output can be increased by "tracking" the sun.

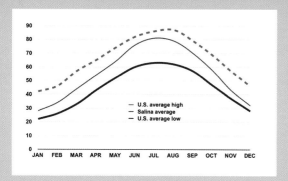

Salina, Kansas, average temperature compared to national average high and low throughout the year

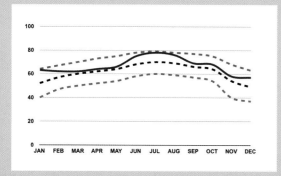

Salina percentage of sunshine compared to national average, high, and low throughout the year

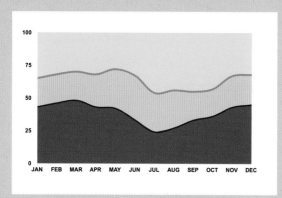

Salina percentage of clear skies, light clouds, and heavy clouds throughout the year

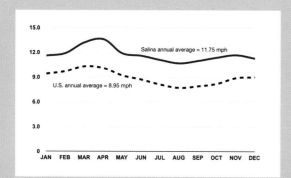

Salina annual and monthly average wind speed compared to the national annual and monthly average

probably needs less, so it all works out. A significant majority of the country would be within 15 percent of the Salina values. As an interesting experiment, I followed the directions of one of the world's leading solar panel manufacturers for estimating energy with identical results to the one I just described and used 25 years ago.

For our example, we will choose a country home near Salina, Kansas, because it has a generally central geographic location, border to border and coast to coast, and has fairly typical and representative seasonal temperatures and weather patterns. The seasonal average temperatures are nearly identical to the national average, with it being a few degrees warmer in summer and cooler in winter. At 39 degrees north latitude, on the summer solstice, June 21, the sun rises at 6:05 am and sets at 8:59 pm for 14 hours and 54 minutes of daylight, and at noon, it will be at an angle of 74 degrees above the earth's surface. Six months later, on the winter solstice, the sun rises at 7:45 am and sets at 5:13 pm for 9 hours and 28 minutes of daylight, and at noon, it will be at an angle of 28 degrees above the earth's surface. The average daylight at the spring and fall equinox is 12 hours and 12 minutes. The difference in the daylight hours between winter and summer is almost 5.5 hours, which is significant.

The sunshine is very average and reaches a peak in July and falls to a low around the beginning of December. The ratio of cloudy, partly cloudy, and clear days not only confirms this but illustrates how very cloudy days are closely associated with precipitation and high wind speeds. Light clouds can reduce solar panel output by about 50 percent, whereas heavy clouds can reduce output by up to 90 percent.

In addition to the seasonal and cloud effects, a solar panel begins to produce power a little after sunrise and the power increases until its peak at noon when the sun is directly overhead. The power begins to fall until before sunset. A simple method of mounting and using solar panels is fixed in place on a home or building, or mounted on the ground. For fixed mounting, it is recommended that the solar panels face within a few degrees of due south at an angle equal to the latitude of the location - in our case 39 degrees latitude. At this angle the sun falls directly on the panel at noon on the spring and fall equinox. A solar panel performs best when the sun's light is directly above the panel. One method to improve performance is to vary the mounting angle of the panels up 15 degrees in winter months and down 15 degrees in summer so the sun is more directly above the panel for each half of the year. An automatic "annual tracking" system that raises and lowers the solar panels to "track" the sun's position at noon each day gives even better performance. An automatic daily tracking system that also tilts each panel towards the sun in the morning and tracks the sun throughout the day gives an even better outcome. An automatic tracking system increases the energy output but is more complex and is better suited to solar panels that are mounted on the ground. For our purposes, we will consider a south facing "fixed" system set at the angle of latitude. It might be noted that the angle of most roofs in the United States is close to or within a reasonable range of the ideal fixed values.

Summarizing, our 2,000-square-foot home needs 790 watts of power to meet our basic electrical needs, plus either 320 watts throughout the year for air conditioning or twice that amount (640 watts) during the six summer months. We can install a 4,800-watt genset and a 640-ampere-hour battery that provides all of our electrical needs. It operates about one-sixth, or 15 to 20 percent, of the time, or 1,460 hours annually. We can run our central air conditioning by increasing the amount of genset run-time by 5 to 20 percent, or an additional 590 hours in the summer months. The total annual genset operating hours equals 2,050.

Solar panels are very simple static devices that simply convert sunlight energy to electricity. There are no exhaust gases or waste heat, and the fuel is free everywhere forever, effectively. Solar panels cost several times as much as a genset, are readily available, and have a long useful life expectancy. Solar panels on the market today typically have 25-year guarantees and proven service experiences in excess of 30 years. Future solar electric panel technology advances will most likely focus on cost, efficiency, expected life, and recyclability as they become less expensive.

The first step is to determine how many solar panels would be required to supply our annual air conditioning power requirement of 320 watts. The manufacturer estimates recommend that we use eight solar panels with a maximum power rating of 1,600 watts, which coincides with the estimate from my method. In doing so, we have eliminated the fuel required to run the genset the extra 5 to 20 percent in the summer for air conditioning and reduced the genset operating time an equal amount, 590 hours. The total annual genset operating time equals 1,460 hours, including air conditioning.

If we add a second module for a total of 3,200 watts, we now have the capability to deliver twice as much power, or 640 watts continuous. This amount of power will take care of 100 percent of the air condi-

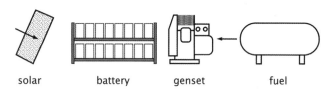

Solar energy added in increasing amounts is beneficial to hybrid electric plant performance.

tioning requirements in the six summer months, plus reduce the genset-operating time and fuel use by 81 percent during the six winter months. Total annual genset operating hours have been reduced to 880.

If we add a third solar module for a total of 4,800 watts, the same maximum power rating as the genset, the continuous solar output is 960 watts. This will provide 100 percent of electrical needs of 790 watts with an additional 170 watts to be applied against the 320-watt air conditioner needs. The genset now has only to supply the balance of the air conditioning power of 150 watts. The total annual genset operating hours become 275. This is 87 percent less than our genset only operating hours and means the genset will last 7.5 times as many years.

If we add the fourth solar module for a total of 6,400 watts, the solar power produced would be equal to 1,280 watts. It would provide all of the 790 watts for the basic electrical, 320 watts for the air conditioning, with 170 watts left over, and the genset would never run for the entire year. Plug in the hybrid electric car!

Now, let's explore another energy source, the wind, to see how it can fit into our hybrid. Like the sun, the fuel is free everywhere and there are no heat losses or exhaust gases. The cost of a highly dependable wind generator with a tower would most likely be somewhere between the genset and the solar panels on a rated power basis. It has been my experience that a properly designed wind generator can operate reliably over a long period of time with very little, if any, maintenance. It can also be easily remanufactured at less cost than a genset and returned to service repeatedly. The key words "operate reliably over a long period of time with very little, if any, maintenance" are an imperative for the design of a wind plant. With material and technology advances over the past 75 years, producing a wind generator that could perform as well as an original Jacobs Model 45 and last as long with so little attention should be easy. Over the past 45 years, I have read most every book, article, and nearly all of the product literature on windmills imaginable. I have also climbed towers short and tall, put up, taken down, and repaired wind generators, and personally steered them into governing winds from the top of the

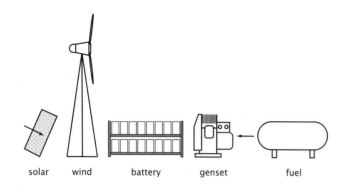

A wind generator adds unique performance benefits to a hybrid electric plant when used alone, with the battery, or with solar modules and/or a genset.

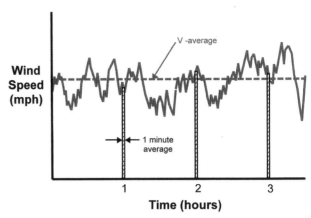

Wind data recording stations take hourly wind speed and direction readings.

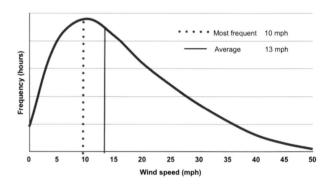

Wind data analysis shows the distribution of wind speed during a year.

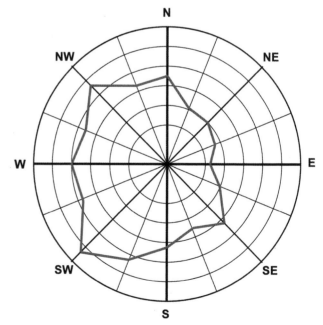

Wind data analysis shows the distribution of wind direction during a year.

tower. From all I have learned, the dependability of the original Jacobs to operate unattended in all wind conditions year after year is unparalleled to this day. Any thing less than that would not be acceptable. Since wind generators with comparable reliability are not commercially available, we can start with a clean sheet of paper and design a perfect wind generator to meet our needs from scratch.

In the United States, weather stations and others have been measuring, recording, and sharing wind speed and direction information from thousands of places around the country over a long period of time. At each site, once an hour the wind speed value is averaged over a one minute period and recorded and the wind direction is noted. For each weather station, a velocity frequency curve can be plotted to show the number of hours at a given wind speed during a given period of time. The annual summary and monthly summaries are the most popular and are reasonably consistent over time for any given site. The wind direction readings can be plotted to show the frequency of the wind from any direction over a period of time in the form of a "wind rose." On a long term basis, year in and year out, we can predict that the wind will blow at any given wind speed for a given amount of time in a given area. We can also predict what percentage of the time it will blow from any direction with reasonable accuracy.

Over a long period of time, a few things can be generally concluded. The average wind speed remains pretty much the same from year to year. The annual average for the United States is 8.95 mph. The prevailing wind direction is from the west across much of the United Sates. The rotation of the earth affects the wind directions from the equator to the poles. Both the average wind speed and the primary wind direction will generally vary from the winter months to the summer months. Local conditions can influence wind patterns also.

Through the years there have been ideas for harnessing the wind with an amazing array of variations on basic principles. A number of excellent books have cataloged these designs and are recommended reading. I have read most of them and, combined with experience, have come to a few basic conclusions about what an ideal wind generator for our hybrid would be. The wind machine would be a horizontal axis design with a "downwind" rotor with three airfoil-type propellers. It would have the performance and dependability of a Jacobs, but would have a basic design similar to the Wind Power Light Co. model.

These choices eliminate a lot of complex science and simplify the technical discussion about how wind energy is converted to electricity. Since we learned about the dynamo, we know that if mechanical energy turns a generator, electricity is produced. The mechanical energy is in this case converted from the energy of the wind by high-speed airfoil-type propellers, sometimes called "blades." The propellers are fixed to a hub rotating about the horizontal center axis. Let's refer to the hub and propellers together as the "rotor."

The kinetic energy in the wind is proportional to the square of how fast the air is moving and its mass (weight). Air weighs more when it's cold and wet. The mechanical power of the rotor is a product of the kinetic energy and the volume of air flowing through the rotor. The volume of air is proportional to the wind speed and the swept area or diameter of the rotor. The result is that the power is proportional to the cube of the wind speed and square of the rotor diameter. The effect being that power is increased eight times when the wind speed is doubled and increased four times when the rotor diameter is doubled.

According to fluid dynamic theory, the maximum power that can be converted is 59.4 percent of the total. The reason for this being primarily that if you could capture all of it, there would be no air exiting the rotor. As it works out, the proportion of how much you can convert is determined by the ratio of the speed of the propeller tip relative to the speed of the wind. The higher the tip speed ratio, the higher the efficiency. A modern high-speed airfoil rotor with tip speed ratios between 5 and 7 feet yield the optimal results and thus convert the greatest amount of energy to electricity of any of the various familiar types of wind machines.

We are ready to begin to design our medium wind generator. As you may have guessed, the electrical power rating is 4,800 watts. Because the power rating is partially determined by the swept area of the rotor, or length of each propeller, and

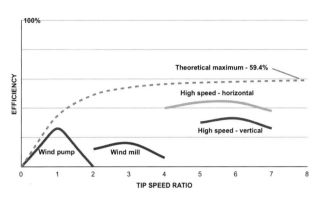

The science of fluid dynamics states that the efficiency of the wind turbine, or propellers, is limited and increases with the tip speed ratio.

partially determined by the wind speed, we have to pick values for each.

If we observe the hourly wind-speed readings and calculate the power at each wind speed, it is clear there is little energy available at very low wind speeds due to low energy content, and at very high wind speeds due to low occurrence. In the chart, although the average wind speed is 13 mph, the most common wind speed is 10 mph. However, if we were to design a wind machine for the most energy, we would optimize performance at about 18 to 20 mph where the most energy is, neglect winds below 8 mph, and limit the output above 25 mph. This is great because a high-speed airfoil-type rotor can be designed to start turning at or near the 8 mph value and can begin to produce power at this point, sometimes referred to as "cut-in" speed. Second, the rotor performance can be easily optimized for 18 to 20 mph (or any other range), and a well-designed governor can limit the rotor speed and thus rated maximum power at any selected point. For our 4,800 watt wind generator, the cut-in wind speed will be 8 mph and the rated speed will be 25 mph, and the rotor diameter will be 17 feet. The wind generator for the small hybrid will have a rotor diameter of 12 feet and a power rating of 2,400 watts. The wind generator for the large hybrid will have a rotor diameter of 24 feet and a power rating of 9,600 watts.

Given these values, we can proceed to make a few more basic design decisions. At any given tip speed ratio, a small rotor will rotate at a higher rpm than a large rotor. Although the speed of the tip of the propeller would be the same, it would have farther to travel to complete each revolution with a larger diameter. Conversely, for a given power rating, a generator becomes larger when it is designed to operate at a slower speed. For small rotors operating at higher speeds, it is practical to direct drive a slower speed generator. At some point, it becomes more practical

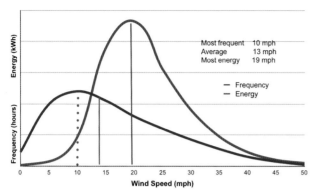

Wind data analysis shows the distribution of wind speed and energy during the year.

to connect a large rotor operating at a slow speed to a small high-speed generator by way of a gear box, which takes some of the power in friction losses to increase rotor speed to match the generator speed. All of our wind machines will have direct-drive generators with the large machine being at the upper limit of practicality. An even larger machine would invariably be gear-driven.

The decision to place the rotor downwind of the orientation axis or center of the tower is based on a couple of inherent advantages. The upwind position places the rotor directly in the wind with a tail mechanism to "aim" it into the wind or to maintain it in an "unstable" condition. The tail also serves to balance the rotor about the orientation or yaw axis to be responsive to changes in wind direction. Placing the rotor downwind eliminates the tail mechanism as the rotor serves to orient itself in a "stable" condition. With a downwind design, the weight of the rotor can be offset by placing the generator ahead of the tower axis so they are balanced as a set and are equally responsive to changes in wind direction.

Another important factor influences my choice in selecting a downwind type design. Let's compare the original Jacobs and Wind Power Light direct-drive wind generators that are representative of the upwind and downwind designs. Both are very successful designs and great machines in their own right. If we look at the rotor from the view of the incoming wind, we would see the swept area that is a large circle on both machines. If we color the portion of the circle that is contributing power green and the portion of the circle that is either not contributing or subtracting power red, we would have a circle with the center one-third red and the outer two-thirds green. For the downwind design, with the generator upwind and fitted with a shroud like the Wind Power Light machine, the wind in the area of red is displaced to the green area where it can be useful. I think this is a good idea.

An additional advantage of a downwind design is

that it is desirable to angle the propellers rearward a small amount. This is called "coning," since it changes the "swept area" from a flat circle to a conical surface shape. It improves the orientation performance, reduces bending stresses in the propellers, and moves the tip of the propeller away from the possibility of striking the tower. A good coning angle, in my opinion, is in the range of 5 to 10 degrees with the maximum value equal to the taper of the freestanding tower.

The disadvantage of a downwind design is that as each propeller passes behind the tower it receives 'disturbed" wind and thus operating conditions change momentarily. A means to reduce this effect and improve orientation performance would be to make the top portion of the tower an aerodynamic yaw post extending from slightly beyond the propeller tip at the lowest point to the generator assembly. The yaw post normally would contain the slip rings, have provisions for service access, and should have a means for fine-leveling the wind machine.

The propeller and hub should have a means to limit the maximum rotor speed by changing the angle of all three blades simultaneously above a selected wind speed. Altering the angle of the blades changes the "lifting" forces of the airfoil section to "drag" forces and the rotor slows down. As it speeds up again in high winds, the process repeats. This is called a governor and it allows the wind turbine to run unattended at its maximum rated speed and output in the most violent storm winds. The principles of the late model Jacobs blade-actuated governor or the Wind Power Light flyball system would work fine. One evening during a powerful thunderstorm, with the wind "howling" and measuring 98 mph, I watched my Jacobs Model 45 governor work brilliantly to limit the speed of the rotor to 250 rpm throughout the whole ordeal - no problem.

The shape of each propeller can be simple or complex, with the more complex designs capable of idealizing performance over a limited range. As such, the propeller can be "tapered" and "twisted" from the base to the tip. The material for propellers used to be wood, namely Douglas fir and Sitka spruce, but would now most likely be high performance plastic or composite. To insure long life, a propeller should have a leading edge capable of withstanding environmental effects of blowing sand, ice, and especially impact, for example from large hail stones in high winds. I also expect that wingtip devices, similar to those on modern aircraft, will find their way onto the tip of wind machine propellers to improve performance in some small measure. In addition, I envision that propeller designs eventually will be customized to the wind

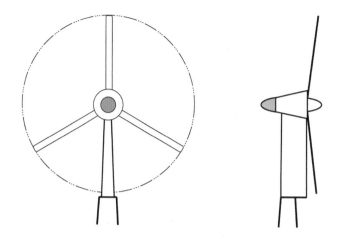

A downwind, three-blade, high speed horizontal axis design with aerodynamic tower section is our preferred wind machine.

characteristics of the region where the wind machine will be used. There are several types of generator designs from which to choose. In the original Jacobs and Wind Power Light designs, the generators were shunt-wound direct current types with brushes carrying the power from the rotating armature. They were designed for slow-speed operations and directly connected to the rotor. Regardless of the type, the generator has to be specific to the rotor speed and power characteristics. Much has changed in generator design from the early days and there are several generator designs that can be used. My choice would be to use a brushless, synchronous, rotating field, 12 lead/3-phase alternator for each of the three machines. A very common design for alternating current generating equipment, it can be externally regulated and has a totally magnetic interface with no wear points and extremely long life. Slow-speed generators normally require more magnets, or "poles," than high-speed generators. The small wind machine may be able to have as few as four but the medium and large machine will most likely require more. In a wind generator, the electric output would be 3-phase alternating current with a frequency that varies with the changes in wind speed. It is easy and efficient to convert or "rectify" the electrical output to direct current for compatibility with the system, plus it fulfills the function of one-way power flow from the wind generator.

Another requirement is the ability to stop the rotor from turning from ground level. This can be accomplished by a disk or external drum brake on the rotor/generator shaft over the tower axis and actuated by a cable/swivel/chain down the center of the tower to an actuating means on the ground, such as a crank handle. Turning the ratcheted crank handle will apply the brake and slow the rotor from

its governed speed to a stopped position and hold it there until released.

The last consideration is to have a tower to hold the wind machine above significant obstructions in the prevailing winds to insure access to smooth flowing winds. I recommend a tower identical to the original Wincharger design. The basic design, including the ease of assembly, the tensioning scheme, and the leveling methods are very practical the way they are. The most popular and logical towers heights would be 50, 60, and 70 feet with the height of the yaw post added to determine the effective height of the wind machine. For example, the effective height of a median wind turbine on a 60-foot tower with the 9-foot yaw post would be 69 feet above the ground.

Since the genset uses fuel and the solar panels are expensive, let's return to our battery system without the genset and solar panels to see how our wind machine fares in meeting our electrical needs. Wind speed plays an important role, and it is important to understand more about it. The annual average wind speed, from all the readings discussed earlier, in the entire United States is about 8.95 mph. If we look at the wind map of the United States, it is clear where wind speeds are higher and where wind energy can be most practical.

From my experiences, I conclude that if the annual average wind speed is above 10 mph, it can be considered an energy source. As the average wind speed increases, the power produced increases exponentially, making it very practical. Below the 10 mph annual average, the practicality of wind power becomes more complex with seasonal variations. At some point not too far below 10 mph, it is simply not practical in my opinion The percentage of places where the annual average wind speed is above 14 mph becomes geographically very small. Therefore, we will focus our evaluation in the 10- to 14-mph range of average wind speeds, which would include all the darker shades of blue on the wind energy map.

Over the years, I have been involved with hundreds of wind generators of various sizes and configurations, and in many cases have had access to the actual power, energy, and associated wind-speed data collected during operation. In order to avoid complex equations with caveats and unrealistic conditions and limitations, I have come up with a useful relationship for estimating energy from a well-designed wind machine similar to ours, but I caution this is a combination of science and sense. In my world, a reasonable wind machine design that uses a fair general rating system will continuously

Wind Generator	Small Hybrid	Medium Hybrid	Large Hybrid
Maximum power (Watts)	2400	4800	9600
Rated voltage (vdc nom.)	48	48	48
Rated current (Amperes)	50	100	200
Rotor diameter (feet)	12	17	24
Rated wind speed (mph)	25	25	25
Maximum rpm (range)	350 to 425	250 to 300	150 to 200
Minimum wind speed (mph)	8	8	8
Minimum rpm (range)	120 to 140	80 to 100	50 to 65

Wind generator ratings and specifications for a small, medium, and large wind generator

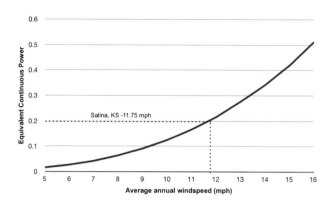

Equivalent continuous power general value is based on average wind speed.

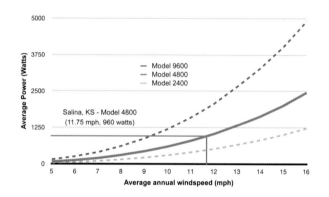

Average power for the small, medium, and large wind generator as a function of average wind speed

produce about one-eighth of its rated output in a 10 mph average wind. At 14 mph, the continuous power output would increase to as much as one third. It is also obvious that at the average national wind speed of 8.95 mph the output is minimal. This corresponds to the lightest regions on the wind map.

For our country house east of Salina, where the annual average wind speed is well above the national average, the average continuous output of the 4,800 watt wind machine in an 11.75 mph average wind would be about one-fifth, or 20 percent, of the wind machine rating, or 960 watts. How great is that? The wind machine will produce 100 percent of our basic electrical needs plus contribute 170 watts to air conditioning. A single solar module with a rating of 1,600 watts will give us the annual average power of 320 watts for the balance of our air conditioning needs with a little left over for our hybrid electric car. The power estimates for the small medium and large wind generators are provided for comparison purposes.

Since all of my evaluations have considered average normal conditions, it is understood that there will be times, hopefully infrequently, that the sun won't shine and the wind won't blow for days and the battery will be empty. There is an easy solution to provide insurance for these rare and troubling occasions - propane. Since we are providing most of our basic electric and air conditioning power from the wind and sun, a small 2,400 watt propane genset could be added for security on these rare occasions, until the sun and wind return.

With space and water heat supplied in a conventional manner by propane fuel in all cases, the hybrid electric plant results for the options considered are:

• The genset-battery hybrid can supply all of our basic electrical and central air conditioning needs. The genset operates 15 to 35 percent of the time and uses a lot of fuel.

• The solar-genset-battery hybrid uses solar modules to increasingly reduce the genset

operating time to a maximum where the solar panels supply all of basic electrical and central air conditioning needs. The genset is rarely used during low-sun periods or high-energy demand.

• A wind-solar-genset-battery hybrid supplies all of our basic electrical and most of our central air conditioning needs with just a wind generator. A solar module supplies the balance of the air conditioning with a little left over. A small genset is included for security all year round.

The result is that we have achieved our goal of a modular family of power plants that can provide between 300 and 2,000 watts on a continuous average basis to meet the basic electrical and central air conditioning needs of most homes and many small businesses.

With the exception of the wind generator, every component in our hybrid system, genset, battery, and solar panel is commercially available today from manufacturers with outstanding quality standards. The wind generator that we have designed could be easily manufactured using standard materials and processes. There are no technology barriers to designing and manufacturing a modern wind turbine that has the dependability of the Jacobs or Wind Power Light machines, and it must have this level of dependability. Any attempt to cut design corners or lower cost that reduces dependability will prove to be detrimental to the success of the business and the viability of the technology.

One thing that we haven't discussed, which can have a significant impact on the performance and efficiency of any of the hybrid configurations, is information and control. Advancements in information and control technology provide a powerful new tool to manage a hybrid electric plant, such as time of day, day of week, day of year satellite weather data and predictions; the actual historic electric supply and use patterns within the hybrid system; and other information can all serve as control inputs. For example, it is a summer weekday and the battery capacity is getting low at 5 am. The genset starts in full knowledge that the sun will be adding energy soon and later in the day the wind is going to pick up with a fast moving low pressure area. With a few simple calculations, the genset makes the determination to run for 1 hour until the solar panels start to produce, rather than to run for 8 hours until the battery is full. The impact of various applied control strategies can optimize solar, reduce fuel costs, improve efficiency and reliability, extend component life and increase investment value.

Another aspect we discussed earlier and need to revisit, since it is the last major remaining impediment to broad-scale use of wind and solar derived electricity, is the need for compatible direct current utilization equipment. Every common appliance or electrical device on the market today is designed to operate on alternating current. Alternating current is required for large central station power plants serving urban areas. The benefits of alternating current are compelling for the generation, transmission, and distribution of electricity. However, there is no firm reason why alternating current should be used in the home. The Delco-Light plant was successful because of the availability of equipment that could operate directly off the battery and genset. I know at first it may sound idealistic to change all the utilization equipment to operate on direct current at my voltage of choice - 48. It is important to note a few things about this issue. For virtually any given task, we can use either direct current or alternating current

for power. For the few circumstances where one or the other would be advantageous there are devices to make the change. As a matter of fact, many common devices convert 120 volt alternating current to low voltage direct current, including computers, printers, and all rechargeable battery powered devices. I recently bought a new high-tech wireless printer that had a box the size of a small brick in the power cord. It converts 120 volts alternating current to 32 volts direct current for the printer to use. If I had a Delco-Light plant, I could just plug it in directly.

The list of the most important items are large in size and small in number, such as the refrigerator and freezer, furnace, air conditioner, clothes washer and dryer, dishwasher, and well pump. When building a new home in the country that will use a hybrid electric plant, the choices are easy. Just buy a well pump, refrigerator, clothes washer and dryer, air conditioner, furnace motor, and a few other personally desirable appliances that operate on 48-volts direct current. It is the total absence of any equipment capable of operating directly on the power produced that is the single largest impediment to using wind and solar electricity.

A solution that is frequently proposed is to buy a device called an inverter to convert the direct current to "usable" alternating current and the problem is solved. This "simple" solution, however, causes problems on many levels. For starters, an inverter system is complicated, more expensive per unit of power than the wind generator or solar panels, incredibly inefficient especially at low-power levels, and completely unnecessary to perform any reasonable task. If that isn't enough, it is very easy to reliably, efficiently, and economically convert from any alternating current voltage to a given direct current voltage. We do it all the time. So the only reasonable solution is that for the benefit of using electricity and all of the energy sources – wind, solar, and conventional sources – it makes sense to begin the process of converting to 48 volts direct current. We can start with rural homes and small towns, and work towards the city. We need some appliance manufacturers, now complaining of slow sales, to step up and create some jobs.

It would be nice if all of the things we have discussed for the household, namely the wind-solar-genset-battery hybrid, also had relevance for homes in small and large cities, and for businesses and industry. Well, it does. So let's see how people not living on farms, in country homes, or remote areas can benefit. We will start with small rural towns with populations of 2,500 or less, and work up.

Chapter 10

COMMUNITY and URBAN USE

The original Kiowa municipal street lighting and water pumping genset

Solving the energy needs of the country homes and working farms does not address all of rural America's energy needs. Small towns are the center of our agricultural economy and provide the commercial support that is vital to the success of our farmers. In addition, they are the vital source of knowledge, community, and friendship in what can be a lonely place at times. One hundred years ago, necessity, along with a fierce determination to work hard and make things better, led to municipal power systems in towns and farm electric plants on each farm. Today the rural electric lines reluctantly bring electricity from far away places as they transmit the town's money away to the same faraway places. It wasn't always like that, and it does not have to stay that way. The journey to rural re-electrification must also consider the needs and aspirations of the small towns. Hybrid farm electric plant technology, in part, can be transferred to serve small communities and make it possible to return to energy self-sufficiency and, more importantly, to keep hard-earned money in town working for everyone's benefit. Our national census divides urban and rural populations at 2,500. The rural population was 23.5 percent in 1990 which is down from 40 percent in 1950, 60 percent in 1900, and 95 percent in 1790 just after the founding of our

nation. In our process, we will start with a median Anytown USA, population of 1,000, and imagine that the household needs are the same like everywhere else, and municipal electric service will be provided to residences, businesses, and a small industrial base that is a source of civic pride.

I was looking through my old technical photos and found a picture of the municipal generating plant for the city of Kiowa, Kansas taken a century ago. The 3-cylinder oil-powered engine and generator set provided street lighting and power for the city's water system. Kiowa, first settled in 1872, was a cattle town near the Oklahoma border. It was the starting point for Carrie Nation's prohibition crusade against the evils of drink and has grown and prospered proudly with time. Over the years, it has added wheat as an important compliment to the established cattle economy. Today, with a population of 1,055, the town thrives in the same proven ways that have served it well over the years, celebrating Progress Days and Labor Day each year with vigor. It is a town that boasts a modern clinic and hospital, library, community center, senior center, schools, churches, local newspaper, theatre, swimming pools and parks, and a history museum to stay connected to its past. Today, electricity is delivered to the town from Alfalfa Electric Cooperative, located 25 miles south in Cherokee, Oklahoma, and the city owns a large new diesel generator set for emergency service. Alfalfa was established in the 1940s as a member-owned non-profit distribution cooperative and thus has no generating capacity. It is a member of Touchstone Energy, which is a national alliance of 560 consumer-owned electric utilities, mostly rural co-operatives.

So let's start with a "new" imaginary town that is like Kiowa and see how portions of our hybrid farm electric plant technology are relevant, and how it can benefit and sustain a rural community. For this exercise, the population of 1,000 people has the same basic electrical and central air conditioning needs as our median family home at 790 watts and 320 watts, respectively. In addition to homes, our city power plant will supply electricity to commerce and industry in the same relative proportions as nationally (37 percent residential, 35 percent commercial, and 28 percent industrial). The commercial sector in our case includes businesses, churches, schools, and municipal and community facilities. With 2.6 persons per household, we have 384 homes requiring 790 watts for basic electric, for a total of 384 x 790/1,000 = 303 kilowatts. Add the air conditioning 320 watts each for a total of 384 x 320/1,000 = 123 kilowatts and a combined total residential demand of 303 + 123 = 426 kilowatts. For the town, the 426 kilowatts residential demand plus 403 kilowatts for commercial and 322 kilowatts for industrial adds up to a total of 1,151 kilowatts. It is important to note that all the homes in our city use natural gas for space and water heating for the same reasons that the hybrid electric plant uses propane.

During the day the power varies from an overnight low, when people are sleeping and business and industry are either closed or operating at a reduced capacity, to an early afternoon peak when power demand is at the maximum before tapering off again in the evening. Annually the power varies seasonally with the peak demand in the heat of summer, when air conditioning is welcome. In spring and fall, power usage is at its lowest before a brief winter increase in demand due to shorter days and colder temperatures.

Since a wind generator on each house in the city is impractical, and it is hard to rationalize each home having a genset, we will chose to use the solar electric and battery components of the hybrid for homes in the city.

From our hybrid power system, we know that our medium solar module, 5-feet high by 24-feet long and rated 1,600 watts, will most likely fit any home in an unshaded area on the roof or ground. The solar panels will meet the air conditioning needs of our 2,000-square-foot home. The beauty of solar air conditioning is that the supply and demand are coincidental. One of the remarkable aspects of producing your own power with wind or solar energy is that a person becomes more aware of both the weather and the way energy is used. The longer days of summer combined with several hours of full output during the hottest part of the day make the solar panel perfect for this task. The result is that the power is produced when it's needed and used directly. The effect on the city power system is to effectively remove the 123 kilowatts for residential air conditioning and the resultant net total is reduced to 1,028 kilowatts.

The battery brings three attributes that can benefit the city electric system. First, a battery can deliver power anytime, even when the municipal electrical supply has been turned off. Second, a battery can supply large amounts of power for short periods of time. Finally, a battery can store electricity or, in other words, accept it at one time to be supplied at a later time. Because we will have more control over the supply of electricity and are not bound by the variability of the wind and sun, we will specify a battery that is one quarter the size of our medium hybrid battery (160 ampere-hours) for our small town home. The solar electric panels on the homes perform at their peak power and have a very positive effect on both the midday and summer demand peaks. In order to appreciate how the battery fits in, we have to look at the primary energy source.

In Kiowa, oil from the nearby oil fields powered their original municipal electric generator. The wells may not be producing like the old days, and natural gas production may be increasing in the future, but the important point to learn here is not the energy source per se, but that it was a "local" energy source. In modern times, we seek new sources of energy to meet our needs. A promising source currently under investigation is in a category called biofuels, essentially renewable solar fuels from plants and animals.

Perhaps a little history diversion may be beneficial. The Ford Model T produced from 1908 to 1927 was fitted with a Holley Model G carburetor. This carburetor allowed the venerable Model T to operate on either gasoline or methanol, commonly known as "alcohol." In modern days, this would be called a "flex-fuel" vehicle, and it was produced 100 years before the term was invented! During this period farm-

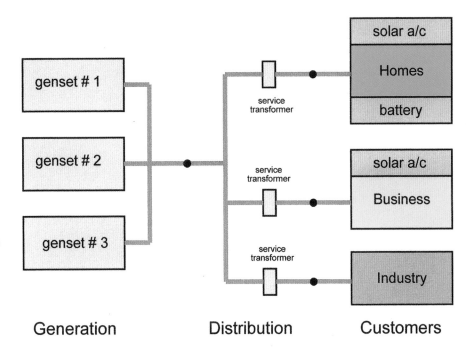

A small community electric power system with three natural gas gensets distributing the power via service transformers to electric customers

Generation   Distribution   Customers

ers had a strong desire to operate tractors and their new automobiles and trucks on grain alcohol, which they produced themselves. It has been inferred that John D. Rockefeller's fervent philanthropic support of the temperance movement leading to the 18th Amendment and Prohibition was motivated more to eliminate competition with his oil empire than to save the souls of wayward imbibers.

Now, I'm thinking that a farming community, with capacity to excel at growing wheat and with 70,000 head of cattle, can put together a reliable source of fuel to generate enough electricity for the nearby town that sustains them, without too much effort I might add. This could be done by using their agricultural mastery to grow it or convert it from cattle manure. Turkey farmers in Minnesota are selling manure at a profit to a company that burns it cleanly to produce electricity to sell at a profit. We are not quite there yet, however, with biofuels. For our immediate purpose, the primary choices are limited to diesel and natural gas. For clean air's sake, as well as the potential of being somewhat local, we will choose natural gas.

Fortunately, two of the world's greatest engine manufacturers, Cummins and Caterpillar, have converted some of their most popular diesel engines to operate on natural gas for stationary power genera-

tion. Interestingly, some of these engines can also operate on landfill and non-landfill biogas and coal mine methane. This is serious equipment with proven reliability not only in transportation but in demanding generation of electricity as a primary source for offshore oil platforms, mines, and industry and a standby source for hospitals, municipal services, and other emergency applications. In addition to being available and reliable, these engines are very clean and capable of meeting the most stringent emissions standards. The sizes vary from the most popular 6-cylinder truck engine, fitted with a turbocharger and after-cooler for efficiency, with electrical ratings beginning at 150 kilowatts, to 12- and 16-cylinder engines with ratings up to 2,000 kilowatts. Rather than choose a single generator with a rating greater than our demand of 1,028 kilowatts, we're going to buy three 410-kilowatt gensets with a combined capacity of 1,230 kilowatts. With a little paralleling switchgear, we can operate one, two, or three gensets to meet the changing demand throughout the day, the day of the week, and the seasons. With a little creativity we can find ways to turn one or more of them off for long periods of time. Just like the engine in our farm hybrid, these large engines operate at lower efficiencies at very high or low speeds or power levels. The operating extremes can also increase maintenance needs and be detrimental to life expectancy. Having the three gensets available allows them to be controlled in an efficient manner to meet demand, distribute operating hours, and also allow for periodic maintenance without service interruption. We will, of course, keep the distribution feeder for emergencies or to sell excess power back to the network for added municipal revenues if we like.

Anytown now has a state-of-the-art generating plant, with three 410 kilowatt, natural gas-powered gensets, serving a community of 384 homes with solar electric panels on the roof and a small 48-volt battery in the basement, the businesses and public buildings, and the local manufacturing industry. An additional benefit to this system is that the users are located close enough to the generators that the genset voltage could be the distribution voltage. The obvious benefit is that there is no transmission network required - no expensive high voltage substations and service transformers - just a regular service transformer at the proper points serving multiple customers. The capacity of the gensets is large enough to handle the average demand with an additional 202 kilowatts, or 18 percent spare capacity, for the peak seasonal or daily demand, and future growth. To ensure an adequate capacity to supply the varying demand at all times, additional measures can be employed, such as finding ways to reduce peak demand; managing the batteries in the residential sector to benefit the seasonal, weekly, and daily capacity; or adding capacity.

Civic and business leaders in Anytown should be progressive-minded and want to find ways to achieve municipal independence and contribute to the national effort for energy self-sufficiency. The commercial sector includes local businesses, churches, and public facilities (schools, libraries, and offices). Nationally, 25 percent of the energy used in the commercial sector is for air conditioning. In the spirit of cooperation, the city and business leaders commit to meeting their commercial air conditioning needs with solar electric, and thus match the contribution of the citizens in their homes. For the commercial sector, the solar electric panels could be connected directly to the building's electrical system. Using a grid connection inverter instead of a battery allows the solar electricity to flow directly into the building, reducing the demand on the generator sets, or if the solar panels are producing more than the building is using, to feed electricity back into the system. If business uses 403 kilowatts on average and reduces that by the air conditioning demand (25 percent), the average commercial demand is reduced by about 101 kilowatts and becomes 302 kilowatts average. What's impressive is that the peak solar electrical production matches the seasonal and daily peak demand exactly. Since the rated capacity of the solar panels is about five-times the continuous rating of 101 kilowatts, or 505 kilowatts, the actual effect during the hot summer afternoon peak could be to eliminate the daily peak and reduce the average demand for the commercial sector.

If we do the same analysis for the 384 homes that use solar electric for their annual air conditioning, a similar result can be achieved. The combined effect of the residential and commercial sectors providing their air conditioning with solar electric can have a very large and disproportional effect on both summer seasonal peak and summer daily peak, plus a significant effect on the winter daily peak. There is an important national lesson to be learned from this.

To make things better, the homes each have a 48-volt, 160 ampere-hour battery that can accept energy at one time and give it back later. From our understanding of weekly and daily use patterns, a few control strategies can be applied. We know that commerce and industry typically operate 16 hours a day, five days a week, and that they have reduced or low power needs overnight and during the weekend. Since our home battery can store power, we have a few helpful options. The first advantage would be that the battery could accept energy overnight, when demand is low, and the battery could give back the energy to the home during the daytime peak hours and thus reduce generator demand by the residential load of 303 kilowatts. Another means would be to store energy in the homes during the off-peak daytime hours in the morning and evening, and use it overnight when commerce and industry are closed and have minimal power needs. In fact, the gensets could be turned off overnight for eight hours on weekdays and a significant portion over the weekend. The battery set's ability to accept and deliver electricity can be used to control the gensets to operate at a constant and most efficient point, improving life. The added capacity of the home batteries, in our case 160 x 48/1,000 x 384 = 2,950 kilowatt hours, can accept the full output of one of the gensets for nearly eight hours.

The combined effect of residential and commercial solar electric air conditioning on peak demand and the ability of the residential battery to accept power at low demand and give it back during high demand can work to significantly reduce or eliminate peak demand. If not, we could easily add extra capacity. The obvious choice would be to increase the percentage of solar electric in the residential and commercial sector. The town could add a fourth genset, and local industry could put in generating or co-generating capacity and contribute. A large 250-kilowatt wind turbine, next to the water tower or by the treatment plant, could also contribute to the water and sewage treatment energy needs and more. In the final analysis, any town could easily formulate an electric supply system for its unique present and future electric energy needs. It is 100 percent likely that any town would not have the same demographics and energy needs as our Anytown, but the citizens, businesses, industries, and public sector could develop a plan to achieve electric self-sufficiency.

This exercise started with a new town, and it is not reasonable to expect an existing town to change things overnight that have taken decades to develop. On the other hand, our history tells us that big changes can occur over time. In 1776, the founding

fathers used wood for heat 28 years after the first coal mine opened. It would be another 76 years before coal surpassed wood for this purpose. In city centers of the early 1900s, people bought "chunks" of coal daily for heating at night. As a toddler, I remember the coal truck pouring coal into our basement "coal bin" so we could toss a shovel full into the furnace periodically during the day when it got cool. When we finally had access to natural gas and converted, it was a giant step forward, and the coal bin became a fruit cellar. Today the use of coal for heat is very rare, while wood has made a small comeback. An orderly process to work towards these goals would normally entail these steps:

• For new house construction, start right by using the 48-volt direct current solar battery hybrid with no grid connection.

• For existing houses, encourage voluntary transition to solar electric air conditioning with a grid inverter connection first, and voluntary transition to a 48-volt direct current battery and use system in the future. The grid could easily adapt to support this. However, there is nothing implicit in the proposed changes that would require anyone to change at all.

• For businesses, encourage voluntary transition to solar electric air conditioning directly or with a grid inverter connection to be compatible with the existing electrical system.

• For industry, look for ways to meet energy needs cost effectively in cooperation with the rest of the community. Independent power producers are welcomed into the supply network everywhere in increasing numbers and with a large measure of success. Think about local energy, electric and thermal needs, and find ways to work in harmony with the community.

In addition to the joy of self-producing electricity, the fact that the revenue from the electric generation stays local can be a great positive for any rural community. Skilled and professional jobs for the next generation of townspeople, additional income for local agricultural products or by-products, and an invigorated local business economy seem like reasonable effects. Using strong technical and marketing experience, I can even imagine the nearby rural electric cooperative hiring several new people to meet the increasing market demand for private and municipal generation equipment, hybrid electric plants, and appliances, even perhaps restructuring as a private for-profit corporation.

Just as we have transferred hybrid technology to small towns, we can transfer a portion of hybrid technology to benefit urban centers as the future unfolds. If you live in a city or metropolitan area, or are a business, chances are you are purchasing electricity from a privately owned public monopoly that has invested without risk for 80 years. What is worse is you really have no choice in the energy source for your electricity, except in a few areas where you have the option of paying more for green energy. The electric company is assured a reward without risk for buying that big expensive nuclear power plant to meet your insatiable demand for energy and grow our economy, but we must make better choices. The best way to ensure excess capacity to meet demand and grow our economy is to reduce the peak daily and seasonal demand by adding solar electric for air conditioning, especially in the southern tier states. Make the money from the next oversized, overpriced central generating facility available for loans to homeowners to invest in two solar modules from the medium hybrid power plant, rated 3,200 watts, mounted on their home and connected to the electric panel for everyone's benefit.

Next, help your commercial customers make the transition to solar air conditioning using the same equipment. The result is a reduction of 16 percent of the residential load and 25 percent of the commercial load for a total system reduction of 15 percent, with industry contributing zero. This means that right off the top there will be 15-percent less wasted heat in the atmosphere, 15 percent less coal exhaust gases, or 15-percent less nuclear fuel waste (or some combination of the two), and finally an increase in spare generating capacity, thus eliminating the need for any new generating facilities for the foreseeable future. And we haven't even considered the 25-percent reduction in overall demand as rural homes and communities make the transition to autonomous solar and wind power, and locally grown, clean burning biofuels for municipal power. We can also include the disproportionately huge power losses associated with the weather-vulnerable rural transmission and distribution networks. The electric utilities that supply major metropolitan areas can concentrate on improving their business practices by actually "serving" the customers in their "service territory" and not their insatiable need to invest recklessly in new unneeded capacity. When they begin to actually serve customers, and the burden of the rural grid is lifted, they might consider burying more power lines in the city as is demanded in most new residential areas. Customers are fed up with hundreds of thousands of homes and businesses losing power for several days after major storms. The "cheap" decision to use overhead lines was a foolish decision. They are ugly, costly to maintain in keeping them free of trees and vegetation, have to be rebuilt after major storms, and are more dangerous.

While we are on the issue of cutting peak demand and increasing spare capacity, a few items come to mind. In our electric-use database, it appears as though 10 percent of the electricity goes to space heating and 9 percent to water heating in our homes. Just like our country homes and rural communities, urban homeowners could save a lot on energy costs by converting to natural gas for these items. A combined total of 19 percent of residential use amounts to a 7 percent reduction of total electrical demand. It would be four times as efficient and thus eliminate three times as much waste heat as the natural gas contributes. Besides, a lot of the electric utilities have been buying up natural gas utilities so the transition will be easy. It just makes sense. Why would an electric and gas utility want to sell you four times as much natural gas converted to electricity to warm your house and water rather than sell you the natural gas directly and avoid putting three times as much in waste heat to the environment?

In the previous two chapters, we have put forth a proposal to meet our electrical needs using a combination of four unique and simple approaches:

1. Rural and remote homes transition back to privately-owned hybrid solar, wind, and/or genset battery electric plants for basic electric and air conditioning

2. Rural communities produce their own power using local and solar energy sources.

3. Urban homes and businesses install solar air conditioning equipment.

4. Rural and urban homes change from electric to gas for space and water heating.

You might ask what the effect would be of doing these things. It may seem complicated, but in the next chapter we will look at how this might play out.

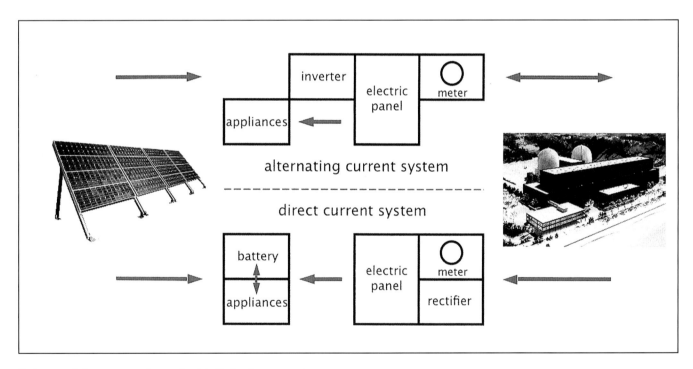

Solar modules can produce electricity for home and commercial use with either an alternating current or direct current system.

Chapter 11

NATIONAL ENERGY IMPACT

The proposed solutions in the previous chapters are actually logical extensions of electric technology development and the pathway to commercialization which began our reliance on electricity. The dominance of central station power that started with the privatization of municipal power systems and put an end to the free enterprise capitalist model of producing equipment to compete in the market to meet consumer demand, like farm electric plants, is a predictable outcome given the principles upon which it is based. Unfortunately, the risk-free monopoly environment that created it predictably led to over-investment in unnecessary capacity and the encouragement of excessive demand and wasteful and inefficient practices through its policies. Let's examine how our electric supply system functioned in 2002.

Applying our definition that electricity is a medium that unites energy sources with work, needs, and wants the proportioned chart shows the flow of energy by way of electricity in the United States. One quadrillion kilowatt-hours is a large amount of energy.

Starting with the energy sources, we consumed 38.2 quadrillion kilowatt-hours of energy, which was 52.4 percent coal, 21.2 percent nuclear, 14.9 percent gas, 6.6 percent hydro, 2.4 percent oil, and 2.4 percent other, plus a little bit imported from Canada. "Other" includes wood, waste, alcohol, geothermal, solar, and wind.

The 38.2 quadrillion kilowatt-hours is converted to 11.9 quadrillion kilowatt-hours of electricity of which 37 percent is supplied to residences, 35 percent to commerce, and 28 percent to industry. The vast majority of the total energy is lost in the conversion, transmission, and distribution of electricity. In this case, 26.3 quadrillion kilowatt-hours, or nearly 69 percent, of the energy winds up as heat and exhaust gases ejected into the atmosphere. Another way to look at it is that only 31 percent of the energy from the source is converted to usable electricity.

All of the heat and exhaust gases ejected into the environment are attributable to energy sources that are used to boil water for the steam cycle, including coal, nuclear, gas, oil, wood, waste, and biogas. It is fair to note that although nuclear energy does not have exhaust gases, it does create deadly radioactive solid wastes that require long-term secure storage. Hydro, wind, and solar do not release any excess heat or exhaust gases into the environment as they use potential, kinetic, and light energy, respectively. If we were to remove hydro from the sources and the resulting electricity, the overall efficiency of just the steam cycle falls nearly 5 percent to 26.3 percent.

The effect of increased use of hydro, wind, and solar would be to significantly increase the electrical conversion efficiency of our entire system by dramatically reducing the wasted heat released into the atmosphere.

As we receive our electricity, we convert it into our specific wants and needs. The residential and commercial sectors convert electricity at an overall efficiency of 75 percent, while industry does a little better at 80 percent. The overall effect is that of the 11.9 quadrillion kilowatt-hours of electricity we are supplied, 2.81 quadrillion kilowatt-hours is lost, and we wind up with 9.09 quadrillion kilowatt-hours as work. Thus, the overall efficiency from the fuel energy to the work is 23.8 percent. Stated in other words, in our electric supply system less than 25 percent of the energy we use ends up meeting our energy needs and 75 percent of the energy goes into the atmosphere. This is not a very good record, but the obvious result of a risk-free monopoly system, which overemphasizes expensive steam generation investment and neglects efficiency, conservation, and user-based energy sources.

When the energy industry thinks of solar and wind energy, they seek out the sunniest deserts and windiest corridors, so they can capture the energy and "distribute" it to customers. It is like they struck another oil or gas well. They do not get it and can't break the fossil fuel mindset. The fact of the matter is that wind energy is available over significant portions of our nation. Another undeniable fact is that solar energy is available over an even larger portion of our nation. Just look at the map. Wind and solar energy are available everywhere and do not need to be distributed. It is delivered to our homes everyday in large and varying amounts. The energy only needs to be converted, stored, and used where it is, which is pretty much everywhere.

The proposals for rural re-electrification, solar air conditioning, and the elimination of electric space and water heating is not a new path to follow. They are the logical extensions of where the electric supply network was headed or should have been headed in the absence of the three critical mistakes resulting in our present network:

• The Rural Electrification Act of 1936

• Overlooking the potential of solar electricity

• Promotion of electric space and water heating and other inefficient practices

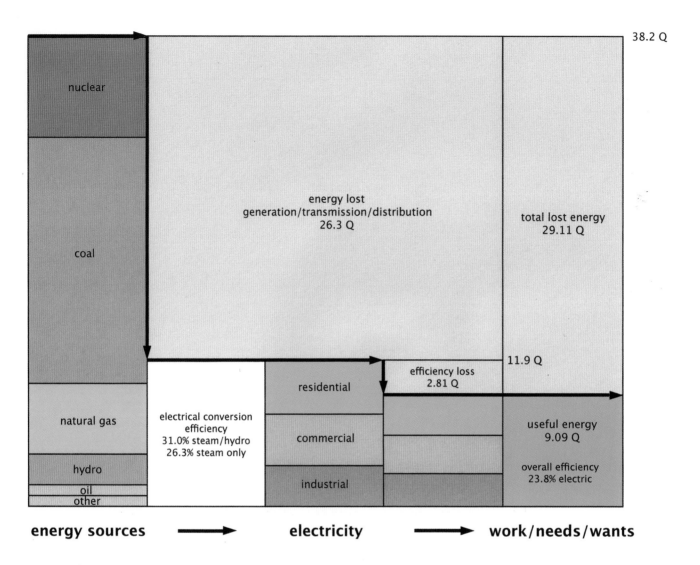

nuclear

coal

natural gas

hydro

oil

other

energy lost
generation/transmission/distribution
26.3 Q

electrical conversion
efficiency
31.0% steam/hydro
26.3% steam only

residential

commercial

industrial

efficiency loss
2.81 Q

38.2 Q

total lost energy
29.11 Q

11.9 Q

useful energy
9.09 Q

overall efficiency
23.8% electric

energy sources ⟶ electricity ⟶ work/needs/wants

Energy flow analysis for electricity in the United States for 2002

So it is fair to ask, what would be the effect if rural areas produced their own power, urban homes and businesses had solar air conditioners, and everyone stopped using electricity for space and water heating in homes? In doing this we have an assumption to put in place. For our rural electrification program we will use wind, solar, and genset derived electricity. The exact percentage of each can vary, but for our purposes we will assume that they provide equal thirds. This is exactly what we have done and the results are dramatic.

The most obvious result is that we have reduced our energy consumption a whopping 24.4 percent from 38.2 quadrillion kilowatt-hours to 28.89 quadrillion kilowatt-hours. Right off the top we have eliminated 33.3 percent, or one third of the waste heat and exhaust gases we presently put into the atmosphere.

A second significant impact is that by moving the electric space and water heating to more efficient lower cost fuels, the overall electric demand for all sectors is reduced by 7 percent from 11.9 quadrillion kilowatt-hours to 11.06 quadrillion kilowatt-hours.

From the energy supply side, we add the assumed equal solar, wind, and genset contributions from rural re-electrification (3 x .921 quadrillion kilowatt-hours, is 2.76 quadrillion kilowatt-hours), plus the solar contribution of urban solar air conditioning for both the residential and commercial sectors (1.21 quadrillion kilowatt-hours). The total contribution would be 3.97 quadrillion kilowatt-hours and, if we remove the genset contribution of 0.921 quadrillion kilowatt hours, the result is that the wind and solar contribution to both the energy source and the amount of electric energy supplied to our sectors is 3.05 quadrillion kilowatt-hours. Thus the solar and wind electric contribution to our electric energy sectors is 27.5 percent (3.05/11.06). It should be noted that this contributes to a reduction in waste heat of 9.84 quadrillion kilowatt-hours (3.05/0.31). Furthermore, this impact increases the efficiency of conversion to electricity to 38.3 percent (11.06/28.87), an improvement of 7.3 percent from the actual 2002 value of 31 percent.

natural gas or other fuel sources the overall efficiency to accomplish all of the original tasks increases to 30.77 percent (8.415+0.675 / 28.87+0.675). (Note: 0.84 quadrillion kilowatt hours for electric space and water heating at 75 percent efficiency = 0.675 quadrillion kilowatt hours.) In doing so, we have not changed the work delivered to society one bit. It is still 9.09 quadrillion kilowatt-hours, 8.415 quadrillion kilowatt-hours electric plus 0.675 quadrillion kilowatt-

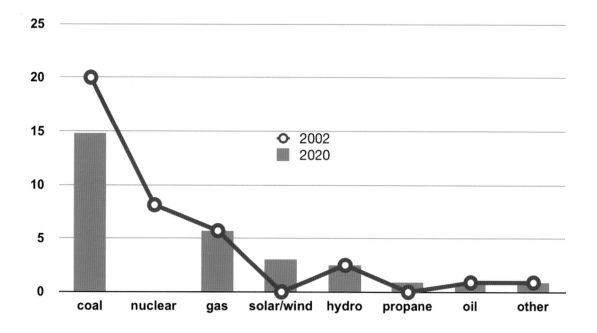

Comparison of fuel use for electric generation in 2002 and with rural re-electrification, solar residential and commercial air conditioning, and direct fuel space and water heating in 2020.

If we continue to use gas, hydro, oil, and other energy sources in the same quantity, the 24.4 percent reduction in wasted heat combined with an increase of 3.05 quadrillion kilowatt hours in wind and solar allow us to eliminate nuclear energy completely and reduce the use of coal by 26 percent. Our new energy mix is 51.2 percent coal, 19.7 percent gas, 10.5 percent wind and solar, 8.7 percent hydro, 3.2 percent propane for the rural genset, 3.1 percent for oil and other sources, 0.00 percent nuclear, and a little bit of imported electricity from Canada.

When we examine the overall numbers, once we have converted our electricity to perform our desired work, we find that the electrical efficiency is 29.15 percent (8.415/28.87), an increase of 5.35 percent from 23.8 percent. If we also include the electric space and water heating that was transferred to

hours for space and water heating. It should be clear that the implications of these changes are significant and dramatic, but look beyond the statistics and we will find a very different society and economy than we presently have.

Since the rural grid is in place, removing it can be accomplished in a voluntary manner over time. For the maximum benefit, the starting point could begin at the most remote points and work inward toward urban areas. The summer home or remote cabin could benefit immediately from hybrid technology. Generally both of these circumstances would have conservative energy needs and could be accomplished at very low cost. Country and farm homes could also make the transition fairly easily as we discussed whether a genset, wind generator, solar panel or some combination of these sources is used.

For large farms with significant electrical needs, the power lines could stay until reasonable local alternatives become available, which I am certain will present themselves in time.

The current economic discussion erroneously uses the "cost per kilowatt-hour" analysis used by power companies to compare generating equipment based on fuel sources for non-grid sources. The correct and appropriate method is based on the increased value of property improvement through investment. Charles Kettering recognized this fact when he introduced the Delco-Light plant. In a newspaper-style announcement headline, "The first organized effort to make electricity available for every farm," the argument is made: "What a Delco-Light outfit will add to your farm investment. What is it that makes one farm more valuable than another in the same locality? Usually it is the amount of labor that has been expended upon it — the amount of improvement built into it."

Since the private country home owner must make an investment and the national network receives the benefit of reducing cost, improving efficiency, and increasing reliability, it's only fair that a mechanism to assist the rural homeowner should be put in place, perhaps through a cash payment or tax credit to disconnect from the electric grid and invest in a hybrid home power plant. The impact of just accomplishing the re-electrification of summer residences, small cabins, country and farm homes would eliminate a large portion of the most remote grid and the costs, losses, potential outages, and visual effects. The poles, towers, wires and transmission equipment could be recycled and made into hybrid power equipment. Everybody wins.

It seems to me that a phenomenon of the American experience is that we have a tendency to focus on the "best" way to do a specific thing and embrace it. In many cases, the best answer to accomplishing a specific objective may be several things: a series of diverse solutions based on more specific varying needs. Nowhere is this more obvious than with electricity. The basic central station technology with which George Westinghouse prevailed over Thomas Edison and the economies of scale have merit and validity for large cities, metropolitan areas, and many mid-size cities. As the city size becomes increasingly smaller, and for areas that are rural or remote, the central station concept ceases to make sense. Placing the rural electrical demands on the central generation, transmission, and distribution system is an unnecessary and extreme burden.

The benefits of rural re-electrification, solar air conditioning, and moving electric space and water heating to fuel demonstrated in our analysis did not take into account the many other effects. With the reduction in transmission and distribution losses to remote areas, the elimination of easements, and perhaps less eminent domain rights of way, the potential to grow and expand the solar electric contribution for a greater part of the residential and commercial electricity in urban areas is well beyond our initial solar air conditioning concept. Moving towards a solar, wind, and biofuel economy along the path we have discussed is the way of the future, and it should be exciting to everyone for a broad range of reasons.

On our journey to rural re-electrification, we have answered affirmative the question, "Can it provide all my energy needs?" On the other hand, I know that if we analyze our work, needs, and wants, and how we fulfill them with electricity, we can do far better. I also know that the path forward involves changes in how we provide and use electricity in a more efficient, reasonable, and beneficial way for people, businesses, and industries that are being served. Investing in generating equipment, learning more, and participating in a national discussion about the best model - business and technical - for supplying electricity in the future is inevitable. I have a few suggestions to consider in closing.

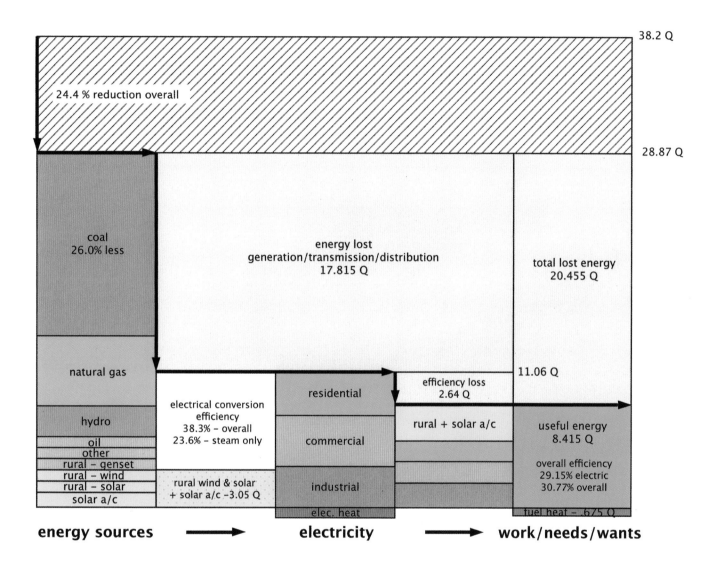

38.2 Q

24.4 % reduction overall

28.87 Q

coal
26.0% less

energy lost
generation/transmission/distribution
17.815 Q

total lost energy
20.455 Q

natural gas

11.06 Q

residential

efficiency loss
2.64 Q

electrical conversion
efficiency
38.3% – overall
23.6% – steam only

rural + solar a/c

hydro

commercial

useful energy
8.415 Q

oil

other

rural – genset

rural – wind

overall efficiency
29.15% electric
30.77% overall

rural – solar

rural wind & solar
+ solar a/c -3.05 Q

industrial

solar a/c

elec. heat

fuel heat – .675 Q

energy sources ➔ **electricity** ➔ **work/needs/wants**

Energy flow analysis for electricity in the United States with rural re-electrification, solar residential and commercial air conditioning, and direct fuel space and water heating.

Chapter 12

NEXT BEST STEPS

The evolution of electricity in our lives sprang from a few simple beginnings of observed physical phenomenon that begged an explanation from a curious scientific mind. The explanation stimulated creative and inventive engineering souls to shape ideas into physical entities and the march of technology into our lives would take another step forward. The contributions of science and engineering icons are not enough in themselves to bring technology the final step forward to commercial products and services that improve the lives of people and enhance society. In most societies a combination of private and public interests in varying degrees inevitably plays a major role in shaping technology towards these ends. The future of electricity in our lives involves these same private and public influences. Our economic and national principles serve as the basis for accomplishing shared goals through the market and ballot. In reality, it is everyone's responsibility to help shape the future consistent with our principles based on common goals for mutual benefit to all - with a profound conscience for our unique and fragile circumstances in the universe.

It was very easy for me, a life-long student of engineering, to understand how electricity came to its present state. It was equally simple to identify mistakes and develop solutions for a more rational and efficient system, one that delivers the same level of electric service to the customer with a dramatic impact on overall energy use and efficiency to the nation.

We have arrived at our present electric supply system over a period of about 100 years. A system that was developed based on incorrect or partially correct axioms, which led to competition instead of cooperation between private and public interests. The results conflict with the interests of serving the "electric customer." The current electric system requires ever increasing amounts of investment in larger, more expensive power plants with the subsequent overcapacity driving the promotion of waste and inefficiency. It is time to reflect on our electric supply network and reform the roles and responsibilities of both the private and public interests to be consistent with our ideals and principles. The effect on the performance and efficiency of our electric supply system could be dramatic.

I like private. I must confess that competition delivers the goods in many cases. I prefer a choice, and I'm a value shopper that frequently chooses the more expensive item. I believe, with justification, that spending a little more on a widget usually results in one that performs better, lasts longer, maintains its value and, in the final analysis, makes better economic sense. I also think that spending a little more rewards excellence in those who choose to build a better mousetrap or provide a better service. There are blatant exceptions to the rule that tarnish the private sector by bending principles and acting counter to the best interests of their customers, but overall our economic system works fairly well.

I also like public. I live in a nice city that serves the residents and businesses well and a state that does likewise, even during troubled times. I think the federal government does a fairly decent job in securing our inalienable rights, providing for our common defense and security, and delivering a range of common services from the mundane to the mandatory to the magnificent - the Hubbell telescope is one of my favorites. When the public sector is functioning thoughtfully and competently, it works pretty well, too. I am also aware that sometimes matters can stray from a reasonable course with the best intentions resulting in unintended negative consequences.

Realistically, the private and public interests have fought each other with vigor as long as I can remember, and the history of the electric supply is a case study in this conflict. The path forward requires cooperation and faithfulness to the principles that guide each. Look around the world, learn from other countries, reflect on our experiences, examine other business models, and redefine the roles and responsibilities of each.

In many countries, the electric supply system is a national public system. A notable example is France where the national electric utility, Electricité de France (EDF), is the sole source of electricity for the entire country, except the city of Strasbourg. It is a very powerful agency who my French friends affectionately refer to as "her majesty." Nuclear energy supplies 80 percent of the nation's electricity, and 100 percent of its nuclear fuel is imported. South Korea, South Africa, Venezuela, Thailand, Taiwan, Saudi Arabia, Portugal, Israel, Ireland, Greece, Peru, and many other countries have nationalized electric utilities as well.

For many years in Canada, provincial public utilities supplied electricity within each province, including Ontario Hydro, Hydro Quebec, BC Hydro, and Saskatchewan Power and Light, among others. Canada's energy sources for electricity are hydropower at 58 percent; coal, oil, and gas at 28 percent; and nuclear at 12 percent. In recent years, it appears as though Canada is trying to bring private interests into the generating sector while maintaining public control of the distribution network. It will be interesting to watch the results over time. I think it is admirable that Canada is willing to seek better solutions to the private-public balance for the benefit of its citizens.

The United States has a complex mix of public and private participation in the electric supply system. Despite recent failed attempts to change long-standing methods through "de-regulation," the country's electric network remains a mix of approaches, which suffer from neglect, and has been overshadowed by financial industry problems. The solution to this is a system that increases private and market forces, including essential competition and risk, and utilizes the public resources in the best possible manner.

For private interests, I recommend a basic paradigm shift from the "selling of electricity" back to the original concept of "investing in electric producing equipment." Every homeowner, business, and industry should invest in electric generating equipment to produce electricity. The original concept of selling electric generating equipment to meet market-driven consumer energy demand is more consistent with the ideals and principles of our economic system. The idea of purchasing electricity from a private supplier without competition or risk just seems antithetical. The defenders of the concept seem to struggle with internal demons when they try to reconcile a private entity and a "natural monopoly." No matter how many times or loudly repeated, it just doesn't connect.

For the rural or urban homeowner, investing in solar panels to provide part or all of their electrical needs is not only possible, but it makes sense by any measure. Rooftop solar panels will produce a steady reliable flow of electricity for decades at no increase in price or use of fuel. They will surely increase the property value of a house or building. Any homeowner can go online, order solar panels, have them installed by a licensed electrician, and be producing energy next week. Start with a single module to get used to producing your own electricity and the performance and add more with time if you choose. With the existing tax credits, especially in the southern states, there is no good reason for homeowners or businesses not to invest in solar panels now. Three solar and wind energy facts for homeowners and businesses to know are:

• Virtually anywhere in the United States, the amount of solar energy landing on a small fraction of the area of a typical home and many retail businesses is more than enough to provide all of the electricity needed.

• Over vast areas of the United States, the amount of wind energy flowing past rural and remote homes and businesses could easily be converted by a reasonably sized wind generator to produce more than enough to provide all of the electricity needed.

• Over even greater areas of the United States, the combination of solar energy and wind energy can provide a steady harmonious stream of energy to produce more than enough to provide all of the electricity needed for homes and many businesses.

Industrial operations, especially those with thermal processes, should invest in their own power plants to save on the cost of electricity or even sell the output during low demand and make a profit on it. Many important business leaders are successfully meeting their companies' electric needs by investing in solar, wind, and biofuel production equipment.

Small towns and communities should seek ways to meet their electrical energy needs by using local energy sources in conjunction with solar and wind. There are many municipal success stories that deserve encouragement not so much for their structure but for their intermediate size and local influence. Every community can benefit from keeping its electric dollars in and around the community.

With the expansion of investment in small and medium-size private power plants by individuals, businesses, and communities, the role of central station electric generation will inevitably come under pressure. The generating facilities are and will continue to be an important part of the electric supply system, especially in large urban and metropolitan areas. I think a little competition and the return of risk will make them a better and more responsible participant. Perhaps the electric utilities will invest in cleaner, more efficient generating equipment in the future rather than just larger and more expensive plants. The obvious benefit to burning less fuel more efficiently is an increase in longevity of the non-renewable fossil fuel energy supplies and a slowing cost increases of a diminishing resource.

The public influence doesn't escape the need to change direction in efforts where competition is impractical, like we do in other essential services, such as water, sewer, gas, highway, railroads, and airports. We should look to our roads and highways as a model for the transmission and distribution of electricity. Private driveways at our homes, businesses, and factories connect with public city streets, county roads, state highways, and the federal interstate system. People and businesses in virtually any kind of vehicle from bicycles and motorcycles to cars and trucks can go anywhere, coast to coast, border to border, and beyond. Although prices vary slightly on a regional basis, any two people stopping at the same gas station are charged the same market-determined price for a unit of energy. Add in a few toll roads and we have the public sector doing what it does best, providing a service to support economic growth where reason dictates a single common solution.

For electric distribution, a local, city, county, metropolitan, or regional publicly-owned utility should manage the distribution of electric power within its area of jurisdiction. Intrastate transmission between larger cities would be the responsibility of each state and the interstate transmission network would logically be the responsibility of the federal government. All consumers and producers would purchase and sell electric energy at a common price. Every private generating facility, from the largest central station plant and industrial power plant to solar electric panels on the roofs of businesses and homes that are connected to the network, is paid the same amount for each unit of energy produced. Every residential, commercial, and industrial consumer of electricity pays the same price for each unit of energy used. Public transmission and distribution networks would also place eminent domain and easement powers where they rightfully belong, in the public sector.

Public involvement needs to be fully evaluated for its merit and suitability. The federal dams and waterway management has been a great technical success and national asset and should remain in the national portfolio in my opinion. The diversion of the electricity produced for preferred customers at cost was a mistake and the practice should be ended. If rural America is re-electrified as proposed, the full output of the dams should go to the electric grid at the same price that privately-generated energy is bought and sold. The profit could go to the interstate electric transmission network, supporting intrastate and local energy distribution, and paying for real energy research, with the remainder applied to the national debt. The aluminum industry will out of economic necessity migrate to the more energy efficient production of secondary or recycled aluminum and raise the recycle rate from 60 percent to a significantly higher level. The end of subsidized hydro electricity for the enrichment of uranium for nuclear energy will most likely lead to the final and long overdue economic collapse of the nuclear power industry. It was a mistake for the public to promote, encourage, and support nuclear technology in the first place. The Atomic Energy Act of 1946 should be replaced with a new Renewable Energy Act and the Price-Anderson Act should be repealed. The civilian nuclear weapons program should be reassigned from the Department of Energy and given independent status and funding. All energy forms should receive fair and equal consideration by the Department of Energy for research and development support, and the budget allocated proportionally to the potential contributions and impacts of each.

A look into the future of rural re-electrification, solar air conditioning, direct heating, competitive private generation, and a public transmission and distribution network will reveal a far different and better electric network. We will see a variety of sizes and types of electric power plants, including large more efficient central stations, and industrial, commercial, and residential systems. The use of solar, wind, and local biofuels will extend the useful life of conventional non-renewable fossil fuels during the transition to full permanent solar reliance. Municipal distribution companies may bury the power lines underground like the water, sewer, and gas lines to beautify every community and city in their service territory. Perhaps they will even offer good advice on how to use electricity wisely and efficiently like the water utilities do. The federal transmission lines could be securely buried along the interstate highways eliminating many of the unsightly transmission corridors. The economic benefit to all segments of society of investing in local solar, wind, and biofuel in all sizes and shapes will be compounded by the environmental impacts and associated effects.

Nikola Tesla is the single most influential scientist and inventor responsible for electricity in the modern world. His 200 patents are the foundation of the intellectual property of the entire electrical industry, such as transformers, alternators, induction motors, X-ray, Doppler radar, poly-phase alternating current, wireless communications, remote control, florescent lights, solar panels, and even the so-called "death ray." His ultimate goal of wireless transmission of electric energy was not realized, but continues to inspire scientific curiosity. The eccentric inventive genius died destitute at 86 years old in his apartment in the New Yorker Hotel surrounded by a city vibrant with electric energy that his inventions brought forth. At a very early point in his career, when the energy to create electricity began its reliance on coal, oil, and gas, Tesla offered this observation: "If we use fuel to get our power we are living on our capital and exhausting it rapidly. This method is barbarous and wantonly wasteful and will have to be stopped in the interest of coming generations."

In our pursuit of new ways to deliver electric power to the people, Tesla's advice is worth thinking about as we go forward and invest wisely.

GLOSSARY

Alternator - A machine capable of converting mechanical energy to alternating current electric energy.

Alternating current - An electric system where electrons flow at an established increasing and decreasing voltage and alternate direction at a constant frequency.

Battery - One or more Voltaic cells.

Battery capacity - The amount of energy capable of being stored in a battery, often measured in ampere-hours.

Central station network - Large electric generating plants that transmit electricity at high voltages over long distances to local distribution networks at intermediate voltages before finally reducing the voltage for use by electric customers.

Current - The amount of electricity moving past a point, expressed in amperes. One ampere equates to 6,443 quadrillion electrons per second.

Direct current - An electric system where the electrons flow in the same direction at a constant voltage.

Energy - The ability or potential to perform work, measured in watt-hours or kilowatt-hours (1,000 watt-hours = 1 kilowatt-hour).

Engine-generator set (genset) - An engine operating on a fuel source directly coupled to a generator to produce electricity.

Farm electric plant - A hybrid electric plant consisting of an engine-generator set and a battery.

Generator - A machine capable of converting mechanical energy to either direct current or alternating current electric energy.

Genset - see Engine-generator set

Hybrid electric plant - An electric power supply system combining two or more primary components with an improved performance over each operating independently. The typical primary components are a battery, engine-generator set, wind generator, and solar panels.

Motor - A machine capable of converting electric energy to mechanical energy.

Power - The rate at which work is accomplished, measured in watts or kilowatts (1 kilowatt = 1,000 watts).

Primary cell - A Voltaic cell in which the chemicals are consumed or irreversibly changed as electric energy is supplied.

Secondary cell - A rechargeable Voltaic cell in which the chemical changes caused by supplying electric energy can be reversed by accepting electric energy from another source.

Solar electric plant - A hybrid electric plant consisting of solar panels and a battery.

Solar panel - A device to convert radiant light energy from the sun to direct current electricity.

Transformer - A device that can change the voltage of alternating current electricity.

Voltage - The electric potential difference between two points. A volt is the potential to move 6,443 quadrillion electrons between two points using one watt per second.

Voltaic cell - A device that converts chemical energy to electric energy - an electrochemical cell.

Wind electric plant - A hybrid electric plant consisting of a wind generator and a battery.

Wind generator - A device used to convert kinetic energy in the wind to direct current electricity.

Work - The accomplishment of a task or actual performance of work, in this text measured in watt-hours, or kilowatt-hours (1 kilowatt-hour = 1,000 watt-hours).

REFERENCES

Abbott I. and A. Von Doenhoff. *Theory of Wing Sections.* New York: Dover Publ., 1959.

Baker, Donald. *Climate of Minnesota Part XIV – Wind Climatology and Wind Power.* St. Paul, Minnesota: University of Minnesota, 1983.

Beedell, Suzanne. *Windmills.* New York: Charles Scribner's Sons, 1975.

Changery, Michael. *Initial Wind Energy Data Assessment Study,* National Oceanic and Atmospheric Administration, Environmental Data Service, National Climatic Center/Research Applied to National Needs, National Science Foundation.

Cycle Change and Wind Turbine Demonstration Project, Newfoundland Telephone Company Ltd. Newfoundland, Canada: Department of Mines and Energy – Government of Newfoundland and Labrador, 1984.

DeHarpporte, Dean. *Northeast and Great Lakes Wind Atlas.* New York: Van Nostrand Reinhold Co., 1983.

Eldridge, Frank R. *Proceedings of the Second Workshop on Wind Energy Conversion Systems,* sponsored by the Energy Research and Development Administration/National Science Foundation. McLean, Virginia: The Mitre Corp., 1975.

-----. *Wind Machines.* McLean, Virginia: The Mitre Corp., 1975.

Energy, Mines and Resources Canada. *Wind Energy Conversion Potential of Remote Communities on the Labrador Coast.* 1985.

Environment Canada/Atmospheric Environment Service. *Canadian Climatic Normals – Wind 1951-1980.* Ontario, Canada, 1982.

Gillis, Christopher. *Windpower.* Atglen, Pennsylvania: Schiffer Publ., 2008.

Golding, E. W. *The Generation of Electricity by Wind Power.* London: Halstad Press, 1995.

Halacy, D. S. *The Coming Age of Solar Energy,* New York: Avon Books, 1963.

Harr, John. *The New Wind Power.* New York: Penguin Books, 1982.

Hewson, E. Wendell. *Wind Power Potential in Selected Areas of Oregon.* Oregon State University Office of Energy Research and Development, 1974.

Inglis, David R. *Wind Power and Other Energy Options.* Ann Arbor, Michigan: The University of Michigan Press, 1978.

King, W. James. *The Development of Electrical Technology in the 19th Century.* Washington, D.C.: Smithsonian Institution, 1962.

Kovarik, Tom, Charles Pipler, and John Hurst. *Wind Energy.* Chicago: Domus Books, 1979.

Lof, George, John Duffie, and Clayton Smith. *World Distribution of Solar Radiation.* Madison, Wisconsin: Solar Energy Laboratory – University of Wisconsin, 1966.

Long-term Energy Report – 1984. Fairbanks, Alaska: Alaska Department of Commerce and Economic Development, 1984.

McGuigan, Dermot. *Harnessing the Wind for Home Energy.* Charlotte, Vermont: Garden Way Publ., 1978.

Near-term High Potential Counties for Small Wind Energy Conversion Devices – Final Report. Prepared for the Solar Energy Research Institute. Springfield, Virginia: NTIS, 1981.

Neill, D. Richard. *Guidebook on Wind Energy Conversion Applications in Hawaii.* Manoa, Hawaii: Hawaii Natural Energy Institute, University of Hawaii, 1982.

Novick, Sheldon. "The Electric Power Industry." *Environment,* 17 [November 1975].

Park, Gerald L. *Windmill Performance in Michigan.* East Lansing, Michigan: Michigan State University, 1984.

Park, Jack. *Simplified Wind Power Systems for Experimenters.* Slymar, California: Helion, 1975.

Park, Jack and John Obermeier. *Common Sense Wind Energy.* State of California, Office of Appropriate Technology, 1981.

Paul, Terrance. *How to Design an Independent Power System.* Nacedah, Wisconsin: Best Energy Systems for Tomorrow, 1981.

Reckard, Matt. *Alaska Wind Energy Handbook.* Fairbanks, Alaska: Alaska Department of Transportation and Public Facilities, 1981.

Remote Area Power Supply Workshop – Canberra 9-10 [May 9, 1983]. National Energy Research, Development and Demonstration Council. Canberra City, Australia: Department of Resources and Energy, 1983.

Reynolds, John. *Windmills and Watermills,* New York: Praeger Publ., 1970.

Ridgeway, James. *The Last Play.* New York: Mentor Books, 1973.

Shuttleworth, John. *Handbook of Homemade Power.* New York: Bantam Books, 1974.

Standard Offers for the Purchase of Power from Qualifying Cogeneration and Small Power Production Facilities, San Francisco: Pacific Gas and Electric Co., 1983.

Stewart, Bill. *Choosing a Wind Power System*. Toronto: Ontario Ministry of Energy, 1984.

Stoner, C. H. *Producing Your Own Power*. Emmaus, Pennsylvania: Rodale Press, 1974.

Sullivan, George. *Wind Power for Your Home*. New York: Cornerstone Library, 1978.

Torrey, Volta. *Wind-Catchers*. Brattleboro, Vermont: The Stephen Greene Press, 1976.

Transition – A Report to the Oregon Energy Council. Prepared by the Office of Energy Research and Planning, Salem, Oregon: Office of the Governor, 1975.

U.S. Congress. House Subcommittee on Energy and Power. *Hearings on the Implementation of the Public Utility Regulatory Policies Act of 1978. Serial No. 96-61*. Washington, D.C.: Government Printing Office, 1980.

U.S. Department of Energy. *Foreign Applications and Export Potential for Wind Energy Systems*. Prepared for the Solar Energy Research Institute, Springfield, Virginia: NTIS, 1982.

_____. *Product Liability and Small Wind Energy Conversion Devices*. Prepared by Robert Noun for the Solar Energy Research Institute. Springfield, Virginia: NTIS, 1981.

_____. *Wind Energy for a Developing World*. Washington, D.C., 1984.

_____. *Wind Energy Resource Atlas – The Northwest Region* [Vol. 1]. Springfield, Virginia, 1980.

_____. *Wind Energy Resource Atlas – Hawaii and Pacific Islands Region* [Vol. 11]. Springfield, Virginia, 1980.

_____. *Wind Energy Resource Atlas – Puerto Rico and U.S. Virgin Islands* [Vol. 12.] Springfield, Virginia, 1980.

_____. *Wind Energy Technology Division. Office of Solar Electric Technologies. Five Year Research Plan 1985 to 1990, Wind Energy Technology: Generating Power from the Wind*. Springfield, Virginia: NTIS, 1985.

_____. *Wind Power for Developing Nations*. Prepared by Amir Mikail for the Solar Energy Research Institute. Springfield, Virginia: NTIS, 1981.

United Nations Conference on New Sources of Energy. Wind Power, New York, 1964.

Wilson, Robert and Peter Lissarman. *Applied Aerodynamics of Wind Power Machines, Research Applied to National Needs*. National Science Foundation. Springfield, Virginia: NTIS, 1974.

Wind Energy Conversion Systems – Workshop Proceedings. Washington, D.C.: National Science Foundation/National Aeronautics and Space Administration, 1973.

Wind Energy Utilization, Cleveland: Lewis Research Center – National Aeronautics and Space Administration, Energy Research and Development Agency, National Science Foundation, 1974.

Zarbin, Earl A. *Roosevelt Dam: A History to 1911*. Phoenix, Arizona: Salt River Project, 1982.

USEFUL WEBSITES

Government

www.eia.doe.gov. U.S. Department of Energy (Energy Information Agency) for national data on energy and electricity.

www.utilityconnection.com. electric, gas and water utility information, national and international.

www.city-data.com. comprehensive weather data for nearly any U.S. city.

www.nasa.gov. U.S. National Aeronautics and Space Administration for information on weather and the solar system.

www.nrel.gov. U.S. National Renewable Energy Laboratory for the latest on renewable energy initiatives.

Historical

www.doctordelco.com for Delco-Light farm electric plants and equipment.

www.wincharger.com for Wincharger, Jacobs and other wind company background.

www.parris-dunn.com for Parris-Dunn history.

www.smokstak.com for antique farm power equipment.

www.hybridelectrichome.com for information on hybrid electric power systems and equipment—past, present, and future— and sharing knowledge and experience.

INDEX

A bachelor wheat farmer named "Slim" relied entirely on his Jacobs Wind Electric Plant throughout his life on the Canadian prairie.